SELF-CONSCIOUSNESS
The Spiritual Human Being

SELF-CONSCIOUSNESS
The Spiritual Human Being

Rudolf Steiner

SteinerBooks

Copyright © 2010 by SteinerBooks
a division of Anthroposophic Press, Inc.
www.steinerbooks.org

Originally published in 1986 by Garber Communications, Inc.

ISBN 978-0-88010-647-4

All rights reserved. No part of this publication may be reproduced, stored in a retrieval system, or transmitted, in any form or by any means, electronic, mechanical, photocopying, recording, or otherwise, without the prior written permission of the publisher.

TABLE OF CONTENTS

Introduction vii
The Reality of Higher Worlds 3
Paths Leading to a Knowledge of Higher Worlds . 37
The Foundations of Spiritual Science 71
Man in the Light of Spiritual Science 103
World-Development in the Light of
    Spiritual Science 141
Jesus or Christ 177
The Necessity for a Renewal of Culture 217
The Relationship of Man with the Cosmos 251
The Soul Life of Man in Relation
    to Higher Worlds 271
The Development of Christian Life in
    Europe: The Mission of the
    Scandinavian Peoples 291
Bibliography 317

INTRODUCTION

THE ten lectures comprising this volume were presented by Rudolf Steiner in Oslo (Christiania), Norway between November 24 and December 4, 1921. The following statement by Guenther Wachsmuth in his book, *The Life and Work of Rudolf Steiner* (page 428), helps place their content in proper perspective and relation to the conditions of the times in Europe, three years after the ending of World War I.

"Between November 23 and December 4, there occurred a series of lectures, courses, and artistic programs in Christiania. A good soil had been prepared here in somewhat more than a decade by the work of active members; and, since the many courses of lectures of Dr. Steiner in Scandinavia before the war, a larger circle of collaborators and also of students and scientists awaited eagerly his first return after the end of the war. The lectures in Christiania of November 23 and 24, upon invitation of the "Pedagogical Association," dealt with *Methods of Instruction and Education on the Basis of Anthroposophy*. Two lectures on November 25 and 26, arranged by students, dealt with the *Reality of the Higher Worlds, The Free Spiritual Status of the Present Time;* and with *Paths to a Knowledge of the Higher Worlds.*

On November 29 there was a lecture to the "Theological Union" on *Jesus or Christ*. A lecture on November 30, upon invitation of the "Economic Association of the State," dealt with *The Cardinal Questions of the Economic Life*. In addition, he gave general introductory public lectures on *The Foundations of Anthroposophy; Evolution of the World in the Light of Anthroposophy;* and *The Necessity for a Renewal of Culture*. For Groups of members in Norway he spoke on the more subtle rhythms in waking and sleeping, in earthly life and cosmic existence, and in his final lecture especially on the spiritual mission of the Scandinavian peoples. Two programs on Eurythmy were presented in the National Theater."

How these lectures fit in with the whole body of Rudolf Steiner's work, particularly at that juncture in his mission and his life, is clearly pointed out in Dr. Wachsmuth's commentary which follows the above quotation:

"This was a unique phenomenon: a single human being in that time invited by teachers, students, theologians, economists, spiritual, social, artistic circles, without regard to boundaries between countries, to provide in all these various realms of life the inspiration for a united renewal of culture on the basis of his unitary substance of knowledge. It was the unique personality of Rudolf Steiner which enjoyed at that time in Europe the confidence of so many persons regardless of all the usual boundaries and differences, and also the capacity for justifying this confidence."

We have titled this book: "Self-Consciousness: The Spiritual Human Being," because we wished to call attention to the importance to be placed on such a reality as consciousness of "The Self," the essence of the free, spiritual, human Being. Steiner himself concentrated more and more on this very point in his writings, lectures and activities towards the end of his life.

Among the very last of his writings, just a few months before his death on March 30, 1925, he wrote these "Leading Thoughts" concerning full, free Self-consciousness:

"Man's lives between death and a new birth also show three distinct periods. In the first of these, he lived entirely within the Hierarchy of the Archai, who prepared, for the physical world, the human form and figure which he was afterwards to bear.

Thus the Archai prepared the human being subsequently to unfold the free Self-consciousness. For this Self-Consciousness can only evolve in beings who can show it forth, in the form and figure which was here created, out of an inner impulse of the soul.

In this we see, how qualities and powers of Mankind, becoming manifest in the present cosmic age, were laid down in the germ in ages long gone by. We see how the Microcosm grows out the the Macrocosm.

In a second period of evolution of the lives between death and a new birth, man entered the domain of the Archangeloi. The germ of his later conscious Selfhood—prepared for, in the first period, in the forming of the human figure—was now implanted in the nature of his soul.

During this second period he was driven by Luciferian and Ahrimanic influences more deeply into the physical than would have happened without their intervention.

In the third period, man enters the domain of the Angeloi, who only wield their influence, however, in the astral body and the Ego. This third period is the present; but what took place in the two former ones still lives on in human evolution and explains the fact that in the nineteenth century—within the age of the Spiritual Soul—man stared into the Spiritual World as into vacant darkness.

In the beginning of the age of the Spiritual Soul, it became the custom to turn attention to the physically spatial greatness of the Universe. Impressed above all by this immensity of physical appearance, men speak of the Earth as a mere speck of dust within the Universe.

To the consciousness of the seer this 'speck of dust,' the Earth, is revealed as the germ and beginning of a new-rising Macrocosm, while the old Macrocosm appears as a thing whose life has died away. For the old Macrocosm had to die, that man might sever himself from it with full Self-consciousness.

In the cosmic present, man partakes: with the Thought-forces that make him free, in the dead Macrocosm; and with the Will-forces, whose essence is concealed from him, in the germinating of this Earth-existence—the Macrocosm newly springing into life.

In Waking life, to experience *himself* in full and free Self-consciousness, man must forego the conscious experience of Reality in its true form, both in his own existence and in that of Nature. Out of the ocean of Reality he lifts himself, that in his shadowed Thoughts he may make his own 'I' his very own in consciousness.

In Sleep, man lives with the life of his environment of Earth, but this very life extinguishes his consciousness of Self.

In Dreaming, there flickers up into half-consciousness the potent World-existence out of which the being of man is woven and from which, in his descent from Spirit-world, he builds his body. In earthly life this World-existence with its potent forces is put to death in man; it dies into the shadows of his Thought. For only so can it become the basis of self-conscious Manhood."

(The above quotations from the book, *Anthroposophical Leading Thoughts* (pages 105-108) by Rudolf Steiner, published by the Anthroposophical Publishing Co., London, 1927. All rights reserved.)

* * * * * *

We wish to thank all those who have helped make this volume possible and we are particularly grateful to the Rudolf Steiner Press, London, for their excellent translations and previous publishing efforts in this area. They have provided the means for many of us here in the United States to first become aware of Rudolf-Steiner and to benefit from his spiritual knowledge, courage and inspiration. We hope this volume will be as helpful to the reader as it has been to us.

BERNARD J. GARBER
October, 1985

SELF-CONSCIOUSNESS
The Spiritual Human Being

THE REALITY OF HIGHER WORLDS

Let me first of all express regret that I am unable to speak to you in your own language. As this is not possible, I must ask to be allowed to deliver the lecture in German.

To begin with, I want to express my heartfelt thanks for the cordial and friendly words of greeting. I only hope that I shall be able, in some measure, to fulfil the task which lies in front of me. I am sincerely grateful for the opportunity given me by the students here to say something about anthroposophical Spiritual Science.* After many long years of work in this domain of knowledge, I know well how difficult it is to make Spiritual Science to some extent intelligible to modern civilisation and culture, and I know, too, how easily misunderstandings arise. For these reasons I want to express very special gratitude to the students by whom the invitation was issued. I attach great importance to the fact that here too, as in other countries, students are beginning to pay some attention to anthroposophical Spiritual Science.

The wish was expressed that this lecture should deal with the theme of the reality of the higher worlds. As all my writings for many, many years have been concerned with answering this very question, you will realise that one brief

---

* This lecture was given in answer to an invitation from an association of students in Christiania. It was held in the largest hall—the "Missionhaus" in Christiania, seating some 2,000 people.

lecture is foredoomed to be both inadequate and incomplete. My endeavour must be to indicate by certain guiding lines, how the higher worlds can become a reality. Obviously I shall be unable to-day—it may be possible to speak more fully elsewhere during the next few days*— to bring before you anything in the nature of convincing proof ; all that I can do is to indicate the lines and directions along which proof may be found. Anthroposophical Spiritual Science cannot speak of the reality of higher worlds without pointing to the paths leading to this reality, and there is no desire whatever to set these paths in opposition to what has been achieved in so admirable a way by the scientific strivings, the scientific spirit of the last few centuries.

It is the conviction of anthroposophical Spiritual Science that doubts cast from one side or another upon the scientific exactitude of its research are based entirely upon misunderstanding. Anthroposophy does not wish to be a matter of amateurish talk but a path of knowledge along which the higher, supersensible worlds are approached with the same scientific exactitude the same methodical and disciplined thought with which natural science has for so long approached the laws of Nature.

If, however, the aim is to reach the supersensible worlds with the same strict exactitude with which natural science reaches its results, it is necessary both in regard to the results themselves and the methods of investigation, to go beyond what is universally recognised as ' scientific ' to-day. Anthroposophical Spiritual

---

* Cp. : *Paths to Knowledge of Higher Worlds.* 26th November, 1921.

Science is founded upon the same fundamental principles which have helped to make modern science great. Modern science has achieved greatness through scrupulous observation of the material world, through experiment, through the reasoned deliberation of what is yielded by sense-observation and experiment. While going beyond the results as well as the actual *modus operandi* of authentic scientific research to-day, anthroposophical Spiritual Science wishes to proceed hand-in-hand with everything that can be learnt from modern research.

This 'going beyond' is founded primarily upon the knowledge that man's power of investigation, in so far as it has developed in the sphere of natural science, comes up against certain boundaries. Every scientific researcher is aware that the great problem concerning the eternal nature of the soul—it is usually known as the problem of immortality, of destiny, in the widest sense, therefore, as the problem of the higher worlds—every scientific researcher is aware that this problem lies beyond the boundaries of modern science. Moreover it is recognised that the whole mode of thinking, the faculty of cognition, the power of knowledge itself, have all been evolved from investigation of the material world of sense and that at a certain point an impassable barrier is reached. Anthroposophy is in complete accord with modern scientists when it is a matter of affirming that these bounaries do indeed exist, so far as the everyday consciousness of man is concerned.

In the realm of philosophy, of course, many endeavours have been made to overstep these boundaries. But nothing that the intellect or the human heart can conjecture about what lies on yonder side of the world of the senses can stand the test of searching examination; the inadequacies of such conjectures are betrayed above all in that they reach into a void. The intellect feels that it is dependent upon what the senses communicate and that whenever it would like to pierce through the tapestry of the material world, no content remains in the field of ordinary consciousness.

Men of deep feeling, who try to justify their needs of soul and spirit before the tribunal of science, who are not content to resign themselves to mere belief but who want to have knowledge of things transcending the temporal—such men are very often apt to-day to take refuge in a kind of mysticism. They believe that what external science is unable to give them is to be found by plunging into the depths of the life of soul. They believe that evidence of the eternal significance of the human soul, of the links connecting the soul with the world of Divine Spirit can stream up from the deep places of the heart.

But with this kind of mysticism no really profound science of the soul can concur, cognisant as it is of all the hidden paths of the human faculty of remembrance, of memory. The ordinary consciousness has, of course, its stores of memories which it calls up again and again because this is necessary for a healthy life of soul. But deep down, mingling with these memories and remembrances, lie many factors which, in their real nature, cannot be surveyed by the ordinary consciousness. Many a mystic unearths from the depths of the soul, things which he regards as revelations from higher worlds, whereas to one possessed of real knowledge they may be merely impressions made upon a long past childhood by the material world of sense.

A genuine investigator knows that what is absorbed unconsciously in early childhood undergoes many metamorphoses and that it can reappear in later life in a different form. Many a man believes that in mystical experience he has discovered a spark of the Divine within him, whereas what he has drawn up from the depths of his soul is nothing else than stimuli received during childhood, appearing in a different form.

These are the two pitfalls lying ahead of us when, in our longing to find the reality of the higher worlds, we embark upon serious and genuine investigation. The true investigator must be on his guard on the one side against a philosophy which tries merely by intellectual deduction and speculation to pierce through the external world of sense to a kind of " Beyond," and, on the other, against a form of mysticism which simply calls up memories in a different garb from the depths of the human heart. In both directions he comes up against insurmountable barriers: on the one side the material world of sense which ordinary consciousness cannot break through, and on the other, the human side, the storehouse of memories which must be present in any healthy life of soul and which forms a boundary interiorly—a boundary which again the ordinary consciousness cannot cross except it be through illusions and fantasies.

The aim of anthroposophical research is to avoid both these pitfalls and to attain true and genuine knowledge of the higher, supersensible worlds. Hence in all honesty and frankness it asserts that the faculties of cognition operating in ordinary life and ordinary science will inevitably come up against these boundaries and are incapable of penetrating through them into the higher worlds. Anthroposophical Spiritual Science therefore sets out to awaken faculties slumbering in the soul of which the ordinary consciousness is unaware, and to embark upon investigation into the reality of higher worlds only when these faculties have undergone due development. This kind of investigation into the things of the Spirit does not take its start from anything that is nebulous or mystical; it takes its start from faculties of ordinary life, but transforms them, makes them essentially different.

The first faculty to which the attention of the bona fide spiritual investigator must be directed is that of remembrance, of memory, within those boundaries and limits of which mention has been made. This faculty of remembrance enables us to call up, either involuntarily or at will, pictures of our life since birth, or rather since a point of time shortly after birth. Unlike ordinary psychology, Anthroposophy takes full account of all the implications here and tries by *deliberate efforts of will* to bring ideas, mental pictures, concepts, thought-content, into the centre of the consciousness—which, in other circumstances, occurs only by the exercise of the faculty of memory and recollection. Anthroposophy sets out to develop a first, elementary faculty of higher knowledge in this way, by means of certain exercises carried out by the faculty of thinking. Anthroposophy does not, however, content itself with the faculty of thinking which comes to expression in ordinary memory, but goes on beyond this—not to the arbitrary meditation often cited by nebulous mysticism, but to inwardly disciplined, systematic meditation.

My task to-day is to indicate the principles of this subject: fuller and more precise details are to be found in my books, *Knowledge of the Higher Worlds and its Attainment*, *An Outline of Occult Science*, and others. It is only possible now to indicate certain fundamental guiding-lines for a study which will have to be pursued for many years. The point of importance is that the faculty of thinking in man is developed to a greater strength and intensity than it possesses in ordinary life and in ordinary science.

When in some piece of work a muscle has to be constantly exerted, its power is strengthened. The would-be spiritual investigator proceeds in the same way with respect to the forces of the soul. He places some mental picture, idea or set of ideas of which he can maintain a complete survey, deliberately and as a free act of will at the centre of his consciousness, and dwells upon it for a certain length of time. Some people will require more time, others less, according to their faculties and their capacity for concentration.

Please note—for it is a very important point—that I am speaking of pictures of which a complete survey can be maintained. If anything from our store of ordinary memories were to be brought up into this meditation or these exercises of thinking, we should be led astray. For the storehouse of thought contains many reminiscences, many unconscious impressions received from life which would have their effect during the exercises. Nothing whatever must be allowed to work from the Unconscious into true anthroposophical meditation; a complete survey must be maintained and everything must be subject to conscious deliberation. Therefore the demand is sometimes made, and with good reason, that one who aims at becoming an actual investigator in Spiritual Science shall ask an already experienced investigator to recommend certain exercises. When such exercises are practised—we may have evolved them ourselves or they may have been given to us—they enter the consciousness as something *new*—like a sense-experience that is not recollected but enters the soul as something quite new. The point of importance is not that we acquire anything from the actual content of the picture or combination of pictures, but that it comes into our consciousness with all the newness and freshness of a sense-experience and that we dwell upon it with our forces of soul. Just as we execute some piece of work by using a muscle, so do we exert the forces of the soul when we dwell upon the picture or idea with sustained and deliberate concentration. If care is taken to observe all the details of the exercises described in my books, there will be no danger of succumbing to anything in the nature of suggestion or auto-suggestion; every moment of the exercise will be filled with a conscious activity of will and after a time we shall feel that the powers of our soul are being strengthened and enhanced.

It is not necessary to devote a great deal of time each day to these exercises but they must be repeated over and over again. One person will need a lengthy period, another may achieve considerable success in a few months; others again will need years. The principle, however, is the same throughout : the forces of soul, the forces of thought, are inwardly strengthened by the exercises, until finally a point is reached where the advance is made to *Imaginative Thinking, Imagination.*

I have called this development ' Imaginative Thinking ' because one becomes aware by degrees that thought is getting free from the abstraction and intellectualism with which it is fraught in ordinary life and ordinary science. Pure thought begins gradually to be lit by a picture-content, warmed through by glowing life, as real in every respect as the pictures and inner vitality produced by external sense-impressions.

It is very important to remember this, for we all of us know that when our attention is directed to external sense-impressions, everything teems, is saturated, has great intensity ; our whole being is given up to these sense-impressions. But if, having turned our attention away from these outer sense-impressions, we engage in the kind of thinking that is usual in ordinary life and science, this thought is colourless, has little warmth. There is good reason for speaking of the colourlessness, the ' pale cast ' of abstract thought. And nearly all the thinking that goes on in ordinary life and science is abstract. Only those thoughts which arise in moments when we are caught up in the outer reality of the world of sense—only those thoughts teem with content. The glowing life and teeming content in what is, at first, a purely inward experience, however, can only be reached by the exercising and strengthening of thought in the way I have indicated. Then we begin, in very truth, to think in pictures, in Imaginations.

But one point must be quite clear. In this Imaginative Thinking we have at first nothing either before us or within us that amounts to external, spiritual reality. The objective significance of this Imaginative Thinking is gradually brought home to us, however, when we grasp the following :—

Everyone knows how in a tiny child the brain develops by degrees into the marvellous organ it eventually becomes in the course of life. It can be said with truth that, to begin with, the brain is a plastic organ, allowing the formative forces of the soul to express themselves in its whole structure, its convolutions and so forth. This process is at work during earliest childhood; it comes to a halt at a certain point—a point reached as a result of natural development and ordinary education. With what has thus been acquired, we try to meet the demands of everyday life, and to make progress in ordinary science. But in that, as children, we have developed from year to year, we have acquired greater and greater capacities.

In striving for Imaginative Knowledge we again become aware of this increasing capacity. We realise that through the activity which consists in the exercising of thought, something that is now plastic within us is being worked upon, elaborated. But we feel, too, that what is thus being worked upon—as it were ploughed and furrowed in the life of soul-and-spirit just like the physical brain in the child—we feel that this is something *supersensible*, something of the nature of soul-and-spirit within the human being which transcends the physical body. After a time we feel that the outer and inner boundaries of knowledge can now be faced in an entirely different way. As a spiritual scientist one has to admit that those who speak of such boundaries do so with good reason, but one also feels that little by little these boundaries of knowledge can actually be crossed with the help of newly developed faculties.

When a man has reached this stage, when he actually feels : now I no longer need to come to a halt within the material world of sense, for now, by means of this living, pictorial thinking, I experience something real when I pierce through the material world and also when I gaze into my own being ; I experience something that is beyond the range of natural science and that mysticism can only call up in illusory form . . . . . When a man has this experience as a result of genuine inner development, he may be sure that he is treading a path which will lead him to the reality of the higher worlds.

To begin with, nothing that can be said to be an external reality lies before the soul ; the old forces have simply been strengthened, intensified. But before long it will be noticed that something very significant is happening in the field of consciousness. An inner tableau arises, encompassing the whole of life since birth. This, indeed, is the first supersensible reality to be experienced : a man's own inner life since birth is presented in a tableau of which complete survey can be maintained. And the result is that the relation of the thinking to what is now an objective perception is different from the relation it previously bore both to external actuality and to inner experiences. In everyday life the human being unfolds the activity of thinking. He thinks about something or other; the thoughts themselves are within the soul—they are subjective. The object is outside. A man feels that his thoughts are separated from what is outside. He now has before him the tableau of his own life of soul since birth. But his thoughts enter as it were into the very tissue of which the tableau is woven; he feels himself to be in and part of it. He feels: now for the first time I am beginning to grasp the reality of my own being; I must yield up my thinking to what thus arises objectively before my consciousness. This, to begin with, constitutes an experience that is fraught with pain; but such experiences are essential and the Spiritual Scientist must not be afraid of having to endure them. I shall speak of this again, in a different connection.

To begin with, this tableau of life causes us to feel our innermost Self under a kind of oppression; the lightness and ease with which, in other circumstances, thoughts, ideas, feelings, impulses of will, wishes and the like, arise, seems to have departed and we feel our own being as it were under a load, constricted. But to put it briefly: in this very experience of oppression we begin to be aware of reality. If there is no sense of oppression, we have merely a thought-edifice, not reality at all. But if we bring into the sphere of this oppression all that was previously within us in the form of freely unfolding thought, we are protected from the danger of illusions, visionary experiences or hallucinations in our Imaginative Knowledge.

It is often said that the exercises recommended by anthroposophical Spiritual Science produce nothing but visions and hallucinations, that they simply bring suppressed nerve-forces to the surface, and that nobody can prove the reality of these higher worlds of which Spiritual Science speaks. Yet anyone who pays attention merely to what I have said to-day, will realise that the path taken by anthroposophical Spiritual Science is the antithesis of all the paths which lead to visions, hallucinations, or mediumship.

Everything that leads to mediumship, to hallucinations or visions, proceeds, fundamentally, from diseased bodily organs which as it were breathe their psycho-spiritual content into the consciousness in a pathological way. All these things lie *below* the level of sense-experience. Imaginative Knowledge, on the contrary, lies in a realm *transcending* sense-perception and is developed from objectivity, not from pathological inner conditions.

To describe as pathological the methods of anthroposophical research denotes complete misunderstanding, for the very reverse is the truth. Because Imaginative Knowledge is attained in full and free consciousness, it is possible to recognise hallucinations and manifestations of mediumship for what they really are. Nobody will reject these psychopathic manifestations more strongly than one who has not, like the visionary, submerged his life of soul in the body, but who has made it free of the body through the efforts described and who is able to survey his own life back to birth, to begin with, in the tableau of which I have spoken.

In this tableau—as I have said, it is a *reality* —we know that we have something consisting, not merely of thoughts, but of the living forces which have been working at the upbuilding of our organism since the beginning of earthly life. The Imagination that has here taken shape is actually the sum-total of the forces by means of which we grow, the sum-total of the forces which work, also, in the process of nourishment.

To what is here discovered as an active, supersensible reality in the being of man, anthroposophical Spiritual Science gives the name of the *ether body*, or the *body of formative forces*.

As you see, a higher member of man's being, a supersensible member which works at the forming of the earthly body, is discovered methodically and systematically. And because in the tableau that has arisen, our thoughts do not roam hither and thither in the wonted fashion but the oppression makes us feel the reality—because of this we realise that what we are there beholding inwardly is none other than the forces working actively in the organism—in other circumstances, unconsciously.

The supersensible ether-body or life-body spoken of by anthroposophical Spiritual Science is not an artificial creation of fantasy; neither is it the antiquated and hypothetical 'life-force' which scientific thought has rightly abandoned. The ether-body is a reality to the now strengthened and enhanced power of thinking—it is a reality just as the external world of sense is reality. And we are led to it, not by any kind of nebulous mysticism but by a strengthening and energising of the normal faculty of thinking which has been enhanced to the level of a free 'I.' Such is the development which brings this first reality before the soul.

But as at this first stage we are simply surveying a tableau of our own earthly life through the flow of time, further progress must be made along the path to the supersensible worlds. This is achieved through exercises whereby yet other powers slumbering in the soul are brought into operation. You all know that in human life, as well as the faculty of remembrance, the capacity to retain ideas and mental pictures, there also exists the capacity to forget. In ordinary life, to our sorrow, forgetting often comes very easily to us. But a man who lives a great deal in the world of thought knows only too well that thoughts can also torment, that effort is needed to get rid of them. This demands very great efforts in the systematic meditation here described, when we are trying to develop deep, inward thinking.

When the consciousness is focussed upon certain images and the forces of this mental presentation are strengthened, the images are loth to take their departure. They press in upon us and allow themselves to be eliminated only when we train ourselves systematically and consciously to do this. If I may speak rather paradoxically, we must as it were train ourselves in a deliberate forgetting, a deliberate elimination of images which want to remain.

In the books mentioned I have described in detail many exercises for strengthening the power of eliminating mental images. When these exercises have been practised for a long time, the point is reached where, in full waking alertness, we can empty our consciousness entirely.

What has here been said is by no means as unessential as might appear. In ordinary life it is the case that efforts to empty the consciousness altogether send most people to sleep after a short time. Now it is even more difficult to empty the consciousness when, as the result of meditation, it has been filled with intensified images. Nevertheless this must be practised. Thereby we succeed little by little in suppressing not only single images, in emptying them out of our consciousness, but, after sustained effort, in effacing the whole tableau of life of which I have spoken. Practically the whole of our life is presented to us in a tableau, as it were in space that has become time, or time that has become space. The exercises gradually give us the power to eliminate the whole of this tableau from our consciousness; it was there before us but we are able now to empty our consciousness and yet to be fully awake and alert.

This is a very important step on the path to the reality of the higher worlds. For when the consciousness, having first been filled with the tableau of life, with perception of the ether-body, has been completely emptied, we are not confronting a void. True, we recognise that the material world of sense is no longer around us . . . it is no more around us than it is in deep, dreamless sleep . . . but a world we have not previously known, a world of supersensible beings and supersensible happenings springs up before us. This is what happens after the life-tableau has been eliminated from our consciousness. It is absurd to say that what springs into view after all these efforts may simply be reminiscences of life, or illusions. Anyone who genuinely experiences it knows that reality is before him as surely as he knows that the external, material world is reality.

The essential point, however, is that when a man becomes prone to hallucinations and visions he loses his ordinary, normal consciousness; he lives in his hallucinations and his powers of thoughtful deliberation have departed. A man who has developed his faculties in the way I have described loses nothing at all of his healthy human reason, none of his powers of thoughtful deliberation. All the faculties that were formerly his, remain, and he can at any moment turn his gaze from the vista of the supersensible worlds before him. Just as he can look back upon a memory, so he can at any moment, and at will, look back to what formed part of his consciousness in ordinary life or in ordinary science. Therefore a man who is developing in this way can fill his whole perception of the supersensible world with conscious thinking, with his thinking that is now permeated with will. He can speak of the supersensible world with the same reasoned clarity and intelligibility with which ordinary science speaks of the material world. And because he describes these higher worlds with normal reasoning powers and scientific method, anyone who exercises the faculty of healthy human intelligence can follow what is said, even if he is not himself an investigator in the anthroposophical sense of the word. This is not necessary, because the true anthroposophical investigator brings the faculty of healthy human reason into play in whatever knowledge he unfolds of the higher worlds. The knowledge he communicates must be in a form that is intelligible at every point to ordinary healthy human reason and discrimination. This holds good not only at the stage of Imaginative Thinking, through which, to begin with, the tableau of earthly life is all that rises up, but it also holds good at the further stage of knowledge of which I have just spoken and have called in my books, *Knowledge through Inspiration*, or *Inspired Knowledge*.

I would ask you not to allow these terms to be a stumbling block. They contain no element of superstition or antiquated tradition, but are used purely in connection with what I have been describing. I speak of 'Inspired Knowledge' because just as the air from the outer world enters the breathing organs as a reality, so does the supersensible world now flow into the world of the soul. Equipped with this Inspired Knowledge, the spiritual investigator is in the following position. He starts out with a normal content and constitution of soul; having once acquired the faculty of emptying his consciousness, it is possible for him to do so again, at will, no matter where he stands, in time or in space, no matter what the content of his consciousness happens to be.

Something is then revealed of the beings and the happenings of the supersensible world. It is like an in-breathing, it is an Inspiration. The spiritual world is breathed into the ordinary world.

Again we must be capable of re-asserting normal consciousness, to judge this spiritual world with normal consciousness. There is a continual out-breathing and in-breathing of the spiritual world, and ever and again the return to ordinary consciousness which enables a man to exercise thoughtful judgment in respect, also, of these spiritual worlds.

What I am now going to say merely by way of comparison, may suggest to you that the use of the term *Inspiration* is justified. The spiritual investigator of to-day is not in a position to press onward to the supersensible worlds in the way that was possible during earlier, prehistoric epochs in the evolution of humanity. The methods by which oriental peoples attained access to the higher worlds in olden times have persisted through tradition and even to-day are still practised over in Asia as a decadent form of Yoga, by men whose bodily constitution differs from ours in the West. Nothing of this kind could be beneficial to the West. It all takes places instinctively, unconsciously, whereas what I have been describing is carried out in full waking consciousness, under complete control of the will.

In a certain respect, nevertheless, something can be learnt from the way in which men strove, in those early epochs of instinctive consciousness, to gain access to the higher worlds and their workings. In the practise of Yoga, the man of ancient India set out to regulate his breathing— to breathe, not in the ordinary way, but deliberately and systematically ; he transformed the ordinary mode of breathing, strove all the time to be fully conscious in and with his breathing, whereas of course ordinary breathing is an unconscious, purely organic process. In that he experienced this rhythm : In-breathing—Out-breathing . . . In-breathing—Out-breathing . . . the pupil of Yoga in olden times was transported into the rhythm of the worlds, of the Cosmos—and in the physical rhythm of the breath he made himself one with the spiritual rhythm of that in-breathing and out-breathing of the spiritual worlds which I have here described in the form in which it is suitable for the West.

In very truth we enter as it were into unison with a rhythm. Our existence as men of Earth can be inspired again and again, continuously, by a higher, supersensible world. What is this supersensible world, in reality?

Through Imaginative Cognition we have learnt to know the *ether-body*, the *body of formative forces* working in us during earthly existence. This body of formative forces has now been suppressed and a new world discovered. The world of sense is no longer immediately present —it is only a remembrance. In this new world, a higher reality is discovered, that higher reality which permeates and works in and through the ether-body or body of formative forces, just as the ether-body in turn permeates the physical body.

Again as the result of deliberate and systematic steps taken along the path to the higher realities and not of any play of fantasy, anthroposophical Spiritual Science speaks of the *astral body* of man which is thus discovered and which permeates the body of formative forces although its life lies in other worlds. And when we examine the worlds in which this astral body lives with the ' I '—just as man lives as a corporeal being among the things of the material world—we discover the world of soul-and-spirit from which the human being descends when through birth or conception, he unites with the physical substance provided by the father and mother. In direct perception —which, as I have said, will stand the test of healthy human reason—the eternal, immortal core of man's being is discovered.

Many people take offence to-day when instead of speaking in generalisations like the pantheists, of an undefined, all-pervading world of Spirit, specific description is given of a world of soul-and-spirit whence man has descended into physical existence through birth and whither he returns on passing through the Gate of Death—a world that is discovered as a reality, not through speculation or nebulous, mystical feeling, but through a strictly disciplined mode of perception. Offence is caused when these worlds are described as I have described them, for example, in my *Outline of Occult Science.* Let me try to explain by means of a simple comparison how it is actually possible to describe these worlds.

Think of your ordinary memory, of your remembrance.—What are you experiencing there? One thing or another has happened to you in the course of life. What has long since become the past, has long ago ceased to be an external reality, stands before you in a memory-picture. From this picture you reconstruct the experience. It passed into you, as it were, from the external world, has become part of the content of your soul. Out of the content of the soul it is possible at any moment to reconstruct the whole world of remembrances, the whole world of external experiences with which existence is interwoven. The inner world is laid hold of, comprised within the life of thought, of feeling, of will. In laying hold of the inner life, the world of external experiences is conjured up before the soul. But what is it that is grasped by means of Imagination and Inspiration?

With Imagination and Inspiration we comprehend not merely what has been absorbed during earthly life, but we comprehend man in his *whole being*. We learn to know how the body of formative forces, remaining as a unity through the whole of life, works in the human organs; how in a world of soul-and-spirit before birth or conception, the astral body bears the eternal core of our being, how this astral body penetrates into and works within us. The whole nature and being of man becomes clearly perceptible. His physical nature is recognised as the product of the Spiritual. Just as we look into our store of remembrances and reconstruct earthly life in pictures, so, when we now look still more deeply inwards, grasping not merely the psycho-spiritual content implanted in the course of ordinary life, but recognising how our organs have been created, how ether-body, astral and 'I' are woven into the physical body—then we can transfer ourselves with opened eyes of soul, into the great arena of cosmic experiences, cosmic happenings, just as remembrances bear us into our ether-body. For man was always present in whatever has come to pass in the universe with which his being is united, be it in the realm of spirit, of soul, or in the physical sphere. And when, in the way described, he beholds himself in his own true being and nature, he can recognise the events whereby his evolution through history and within the Cosmos has been made possible.

Those who grasp the full import of these thoughts will no longer consider it peculiar when, in my *Outline of Occult Science*, they find descriptions of how the human being, in his primeval forms, was connected not only with the Earth but with planetary worlds which, as earlier metamorphoses, preceded the Earth, and how the very make-up and constitution of the human being points to future transformations of the Earth into other planetary conditions; how it is possible really to penetrate into higher worlds and to recognise the kingdoms around us as men of Earth as the product of higher, spiritual worlds, supersensible worlds.

It is only right that the strenuous efforts which anthroposophical Spiritual Science must make to achieve these results should be known and understood. There is a very prevalent opinion that what spiritual research says about the reality of higher worlds is merely the result of some form of 'inspiration,' so-called, or of subjective, intellectual deduction, or even of pure fantasy. Indeed it is not so. Clinical research, astronomical research, for example, demands specialised and difficult work. But what is acquired inwardly in the way described, learnt as it were from man's own being by inner experimentation in order to unfold perception of higher worlds—this is an even more difficult task, demanding greater devotion, greater care, greater exactitude and methodical perseverance. What is here described in all seriousness as Spiritual Science is fundamentally different from current forms of Occultism, Mysticism and the like. As science stands in contrast with superstition, so does anthroposophical Spiritual Science stand in contrast with current forms of Occultism which try to acquire knowledge through mediums or by compiling external, sensational data in amateurish fashion. This particular brand of modern superstition is vanquished by nothing more decisively than by genuine spiritual research, with its absolutely scrupulous and exact methods.

When, having acquired Knowledge through Inspiration, a man is able to gaze into the world he left at birth or conception and will enter again after death, he experiences something which in its reflection in the ordinary consciousness seems to be a kind of pessimism.—In the realm of ordinary consciousness, after all, anything supersensible assumes the form of indefinite, inchoate feelings and the like.—The experiences which come to the spiritual investigator through Inspiration seem to take the form of pessimism. Why pessimism ? Because it is actually the case that when the spiritual investigator enters the higher worlds, he experiences something like deep pain, universal privation.

By means of the exercises indicated in my books, we must be armed against this pain, be ready to bear it valiantly and resolutely. What, then, is this pain that is experienced in all reality ? It is actually a deep and intense longing, it is none other than experience of that force whereby the soul passes from the spiritual worlds through birth into physical existence. The soul has been living in spiritual worlds, and the last period of this life, before the descent through birth into physical existence, is experienced as a yearning for the physical world. This yearning subsequently becomes the pain experienced by the spiritual investigator. And precisely because experiences in the realm of Spiritual Science are not abstract or theoretical and because the whole being of man is involved, including his feeling and willing, this pain is an essential part of the path leading into the higher worlds.

Theorising is by no means sufficient when it is a matter of treading the anthroposophical path into the spiritual worlds. The experiences which accompany the methods employed by genuine investigation demand, at every stage, due moral preparation. And there is really no better preparation for the moral strengthening of man in body, soul and spirit, than practise of the exercises leading to knowledge of the reality of the higher worlds. They will never reveal themselves to one who merely theorises, but only to one who devotes his whole manhood to quickening in the soul all his faculties of good feeling, of appreciation of beauty in the world, his power of reverent contemplation of the secrets of the Universe. Only he who makes love of men and love of worlds into forces of inner, all-permeating warmth, achieves the moral strength that is necessary in order to press forward to the reality of higher worlds.

Many will admit, therefore, that the exercises I describe for the path to the higher worlds taken by Spiritual Science, have a moral side that is genuinely worthy of recognition. This will be admitted, too, by those who fall away and are not willing to tread the actual path to knowledge of the higher worlds. Yet it is this path alone which, in face of the modern longing for science, can lead into these worlds.

Through Imagination and Inspiration a man reaches his innermost Self. But this innermost Self must also surrender itself to the world around. I have already explained that thinking, even at the stage of Imagination, must flow outwards, into what is objective. Thinking, deliberate and disciplined thinking, is always in operation in our discovery of higher worlds; but we must also be aware that our whole being has, as it were, to be given over to this reality of the supersensible worlds. After the attainment of Inspiration, however, through the efforts made and the experiences undergone, we become aware of the 'I,' the central core of our being, in all intensity. And this is the point at which the harmony, the union between the experience of freedom and that of nature-necessity can be realised and known.

In ordinary life we are enclosed in the web of this nature-necessity. How often we feel that what is living in our impulses of will surges up from subconscious depths, from instincts and natural urges, even when it has worked itself a little way out of the sinful in the direction of the good. It is almost as impossible to survey what is working in the urges and impulses of the will as it is to survey the experiences undergone during sleep. And after all, in the urges and impulses of the will, there is contained much that plays into our life of conscious, moral responsibility.

A man who has achieved Inspiration and Imagination however, has been strengthened by his efforts and exertions. He experiences the ' I ' in far greater intensity—given over to the world, it is true, yet restored to his keeping. Such a man will not say with those who adhere to prejudiced scientific views : the same nature-necessity which causes the stone to fall to the ground, the stone in turn to be warmed by the sun, the nature-necessity which inheres in electricity, in magnetism, in acoustic and optical phenomena—that same necessity is at work when, as a human being, I act and unfold my impulses of will. Indeed in ordinary science and everyday life men cannot get rid of the gnawing doubts which assail them in connection with this problem.

On the one side there is the reality of human freedom. But the conviction is prevalent that this freedom must be renounced if one is a scientist in the modern sense, believing in the conservation of energy and matter and holding the view that no impulse of the human will, no human action can emanate from free will, since man, in common with all other creatures in the kingdoms of nature, must be subject to the domination of nature-necessity.

But with his true ' I ' before him in greater strength and intensity, man acquires a kind of knowledge still higher than Inspiration and Imagination. I have called this still higher form of knowledge, true *Intuition*, for it denotes complete mergence in spiritual reality. At this stage, the fact of man's repeated earthly lives spoken of by Anthroposophy is filled with meaning. The necessity which seems to be implicit in a man's actions, in his will, is recognised as the consequence of preceding lives on Earth. Man's eternal core of being passes through repeated earthly lives, and between these lives—that is to say, between death and a new birth—leads an existence in worlds of soul and spirit. And now comes the knowledge : flowing from life to life there is the factor which entails subjection of the ' I ' together with its impulses of will . . . *not*, however, to external, nature-necessity but to the necessity which runs through the chain of earthly lives.

To begin with, this necessity is hidden from ordinary thinking. But when truly free, sense-free thinking as described in my *Philosophy of Spiritual Activity* is unfolded in a single earth-existence—with this kind of thinking we have the real foundation of our freedom, our free spiritual activity. In that we rise, as man, to these moral impulses which are seized by the free power of thought, we become free human beings here on the Earth. And what inheres in our existence in the form of necessity, living itself out as destiny—this is not nature-necessity but the necessity which runs through repeated earthly lives.

This too is revealed to *Intuition*, the third stage of supersensible knowledge. There before us, presented in wonderful harmony, is the freedom inherent in a single earthly life, and what we feel to be the necessity of destiny—which is not external, nature-necessity, nor due to the normal constitution of the human body, but which streams in from earlier earthly lives. This no more makes us unfree than does a change of the stage on which our life takes its course, when circumstances are such as to make us still dependent upon the connection between this new life and the old.—If for example, we emigrate from Europe to America, the ship takes us thither and our life proceeds in a new setting. This is destiny; but in spite of having crossed from Europe to America, we remain free beings. Necessity and freedom can be differentiated when we perceive on the one side the necessity inhering in repeated earthly lives and, on the other, the freedom which is implicit in each single earthly life.

To look upwards into the higher worlds gives us security and confidence inasmuch as the purpose and meaning of earthly life become clear. We no longer merely yearn for higher worlds—although that too is necessary for any sense of security on the Earth. Earthly life becomes insecure if we lose our connection with the Divine-Spiritual within us.

True anthroposophical knowledge of the reality of higher worlds does not estrange us from the affairs of the Earth : we know that the descent to the Earth must be made over and over again in order that freedom may become an integral part of man's estate. Conscious realisation of freedom permeates us in spite of our realisation of the problems of destiny, for we have learnt to understand these problems in their spiritual aspect, in the light of the reality of the higher worlds.

It has only been possible to give a very bare outline of this subject. Abundant literature exists to-day and is at the disposal of everybody. In one brief lecture I have only been able to indicate certain guiding lines, but what has been said will to some extent show you that anthroposophical knowledge of the supersensible worlds has not the slightest tendency to be remote from the world, to be unpractical. It does not wish to lead human beings in their egotism into vapid castles in the air ; on the contrary, it holds that to alienate a man from the world would be to sin against the Spiritual. The Spirit is only truly within our grasp when the flow of its power makes us practical and capable human beings.

The Spirit is *creative ;* the mission of the Spirit is to permeate, not to escape from material existence. Anthroposophical knowledge of the supersensible worlds is therefore at the same time a power in practical life. Hence—as I shall show in other lectures here in Christiania—Anthroposophy strives to enrich the several sciences, the life of art, as well the domains of practical life, with all that knowledge of the reality of higher worlds can add to the things of the material world.

As we have heard, Imaginative Knowledge reveals the ether-body, the body of formative forces. When, in the light of this knowledge, we understand the nature of the human bodily organisation, when we understand how the astral body which has descended from worlds of soul-and-spirit, works in man as an earthly being, in lung, liver, stomach, brain, and so forth . . . then we understand the nature of health and illness. When this point is reached, our realisation of the higher worlds will have succeeded not merely in satisfying a need of knowledge, but actually in enriching medicine and therapy. In Stuttgart and in Dornach we already have clinics and institutes engaged in the practical application of the contributions which anthroposophical knowledge can make to medicine, to therapy—especially to therapy—but also to pathology. Anthroposophy strives, too, to make this knowledge of higher worlds bear fruit in the realm of art.

In the Goetheanum Building at Dornach, in the High School for Spiritual Science, a new style of architecture was created*, out of anthroposophical principles. This new style of architecture has no sort of tendency towards the symbolic or the allegoric. Not a single symbol, not a single allegorical form will be found there; everything is the product of creative art in the truest sense. Spiritual Science is *not* theory, it is not a matter merely of the intellect. The element of intellect dragged down into art would produce nothing but barren, allegorical symbolism, Spiritual Science leads to actual perception, to concrete understanding of the spiritual world. The content of

---

* See: *Ways to a New Style in Architecture* (with 12 illustrations of the first Goetheanum), by Rudolf Steiner.

the spiritual world can then be woven into the material world. In the highest degree we strive to fulfil Goethe's demand, namely, that Art should be a manifestation of secret laws of Nature which, without her, could never bear fruit. And we are also endeavouring to develop an art of movement founded on the reality of the formative forces working supersensibly within the human being. This is Eurhythmy, a performance of which is to be given here next Sunday.

Eurhythmy is not an art of dancing, nor anything in the nature of mime; it is an art that has been brought down from the supersensible into the material domain of man's being; it gives expression to the intimate connection of the human being with the Cosmos and its laws, showing how in a 'visible speech,' secrets of the life of soul and spirit can be made manifest, as well as in audible speech or song.

Similarly, Spiritual Science can flow into the social life, the moral and ethical life. I have tried to show this in my book, *The Threefold Commonwealth*. The problems of the social life of men can never be adequately solved by Marxian or other materialistic theories. In his innermost existence man is a spiritual, supersensible being, and as a social being, too, it is his task to give expression to the supersensible in the domain of his social life. Failing this, the burning social questions of our time can never be fruitfully solved.

Finally, the path to higher worlds which anthroposophical Spiritual Science strives to tread by means of genuine research and not through mere belief—this path is connected with man's deepest and most inward quest, with the bonds he tries in devotion and piety to forge with the Divine-Spiritual foundations of the Universe. In short, Spiritual Science is bound up with the deepest religious feelings arising in the human heart, with the religious life that must unfold if the true dignity of manhood is to be attained. And so anthroposophical knowledge of the supersensible worlds is at the same time a quickening, an enrichment of the religious life, of which, as every unprejudiced mind will admit, we stand in dire need to-day.

It is well-nigh incomprehensible to me that again, quite recently, anthroposophical Spiritual Science should have been accused by theological circles of destroying the religious life. It has been said, for example : the life of Anthroposophy betokens the death of religion ! Now the life of Anthroposophy is indissolubly bound up with that life of the soul in which the very deepest forces of religion unfold. This search for supersensible realities cannot betoken the death of religion—at most it might betoken the end of something that is merely regarded as religion and is already dead. If, indeed, this is what has happened to religion, Anthroposophy would simply be opening up a vista of death. By its very nature, however, being a living path to the supersensible realities, Anthroposophy is a means whereby the religious feelings, the whole-hearted devotion of men to the supersensible worlds may be enhanced, quickened, pervaded with warmth*.

The goal of Anthroposophy is to work fruitfully in all the different spheres of life, from the secular to the most sacred. In the noblest sense—

---

* Compare : *Jesus or Christ*, a lecture given by invitation in the Theolog. Verein, Christiania, 29th November, 1921.

however far off achievement still lies to-day—the goal and ideal of Anthroposophy is to promote and be a real factor in the advancing evolution of mankind. And every unprejudiced person who has passed with alert consciousness through the catastrophic period of the second decade of the twentieth century, will admit that many, many spheres of existence to-day are calling out for new and vitalising impulses.

What I have put before you in such brief outline is connected with the eternal concerns of human life. Anthroposophy can be cultivated in the forum of life, where man does not always seem to demand that inner security which can only be found in consciousness of his eternal being ; and it can be cultivated in quietude, away from the hubbub of the forum of life. The human being of every epoch must be in contact with the Eternal within him, if he would be truly Man. Thus Anthroposophy is of universal, vital interest to all men because it concerns the things that are Eternal in human existence. In our days, when the signs of decline are to be seen on every hand, it must surely be admitted, too, that there is need to counter the forces of decline with impulses for the ennobling of Western civilisation. Anthroposophy is worthy of attention to-day not only because it pays heed to the Eternal but also because of the difficult tasks confronting our times.

In conclusion, let me say this.—Unlike the current tendency to lead the human being to mystical castles in the air and thus to estrangement from the world, the aim of Anthroposophy is to lead him to the reality of the supersensible worlds in such a way that having seized the Spirit he may take a real hand in the affairs of practical and material life. In very truth man must lay hold of the Spirit, for the reason that if his life is to rest upon sure foundations, contact with the supersensible worlds and with the Eternal part of his being is all-essential. And nowadays, above all, man needs the Spirit for the solving of the hard and heavy problems which surround him in these catastrophic times.

PATHS LEADING TO A KNOWLEDGE OF HIGHER WORLDS

I have been asked to speak to-day on the subject: Paths leading to higher, that is to supersensible knowledge. As not all of you were present at my last lecture, it will be necessary to weave into this lecture some of the more important things explained yesterday.

The spiritual science of Anthroposophy strives above all towards a full harmony with the scientific truths which have emerged in the course of the past centuries. Anthroposophy is in no way directed *against* the efforts of natural science, as so many people believe; on the contrary, those who honestly and earnestly stand within our anthroposophical movement appreciate most of all such men as can fully judge the achievement of our modern times, resulting from scientific conscientiousness, from inner scientific feeling. It is however true that one cannot penetrate into the supersensible worlds with the aid of the generally accepted science, and in regard to this point Anthroposophy in a certain way shares the views of the officially recognised scientists.

Anthroposophy clearly recognises that people are quite right when in regard to natural science they speak of boundaries to human knowledge. Anthroposophy also recognises that one cannot step beyond these boundaries with the ordinary forces of human understanding. Consequently Anthroposophy does not even attempt to discover paths to supersensible knowledge by applying the forces of ordinary consciousness and ordinary knowledge, but it strives not only as regards the results of scientific investigation to begin where ordinary science must come to an end, but through its methods Anthroposophy also strives to begin where the generally accepted science must come to a final point in regard to a knowledge of external Nature and also of the physical nature of the human being.

Consequently Anthroposophy must not only speak of different subjects, but it must also speak in a different way. Nevertheless it is in full harmony with scientific conscientiousness and scientific discipline. Its starting point is to draw out of man's inner being latent forces, to rouse slumbering forces of knowledge enabling the human being to penetrate into the supersensible worlds.

Anthroposophy does not say that special qualities and capacities are needed for a knowledge of the supersensible worlds, it does not declare that such a knowledge is based on qualities which can only be possessed by a few people, but it takes as its foundation forces which can be drawn out of every human soul, forces which transcend those which we inherit, as it were, from childhood onwards and which also transcend those which we gain through ordinary education, through an ordinary schooling.

A person who wishes to become a spiritual investigator, in the anthroposophical sense of this word, must set out from the point where he stands in ordinary life and in ordinary science; from there he must guide his development of his own accord. The forces which should be developed first of all, are the forces of thinking. This is a first step in such a development, and we shall see that this does not imply the development of one-sided intellectual forces of thought, but the unfolding of the whole human being. But a beginning must be made with a particular exercise in thinking.

The kind of thinking to which we are accustomed in ordinary life and also in ordinary science is given up to external observation and follows, as it were, the thread of external observation. We direct our senses towards the external world and link our thoughts with perceptions transmitted by the senses. The observation of the external world provides a firm support, enabling us to connect our experiences with the contents of our soul.

It has been the endeavour of science, and rightly so, to develop more and more the support given by external observation. Observation has been enhanced by the use of scientific experimental research, where every single condition leading to different manifestations can be clearly surveyed, so that the processes become, as it were, quite transparent.

For the attainment of its task, the spiritual science of Anthroposophy must deviate from this way of thinking which is entirely directed towards the objective reality outside. Anthroposophy must above all strengthen and intensify thought within the human being. In the public lecture which I gave yesterday I remarked that a muscle grows stronger if it does a certain work and that the same applies to the forces of the soul. When certain definite concepts which can easily be surveyed are again and again set at the centre of our consciousness by systematic practice, so that we completely surrender to such concepts, our thinking power grows stronger.

This intensification of the forces of thinking must of course be reached in such a way as to maintain throughout our clear and complete will-power. A person who wishes to become a spiritual investigator in the anthroposophical sense, may therefore take mathematics above all as an excellent example for the scientific mentality of modern times.

Though it may sound strange and paradoxical it must be said that an anthroposophical spiritual investigator who wishes to transcend the stage of dilettantism, must in the first place observe a rule which already existed in the old Platonic school : That no one can penetrate into real spiritual-scientific knowledge unless he has a certain mathematical culture.

What particular result can the human soul gain through mathematics ? The result that everything which confronts the soul through mathematics can be inwardly surveyed, is inwardly transparent, and that mathematics contains, as it were, nothing to which we submit unconsciously, without the application of our will.

The spiritual science of Anthroposophy is naturally not mathematics. But a significant example may be found in the way in which one penetrates into mathematical thought. It is not mathematics in itself which constitutes this example, but—if I may coin this expression,—"mathematizing," the activity of mathematical thinking. If such a "mathematizing" culture shows us how to transcend any illusionary or suggestive element, we shall be particularly successful in concentrating upon concepts which can be surveyed and which are quite new to us.

Such concepts can be obtained from an experienced spiritual-scientific investigator, or in some other way we may seek to develop concepts which do not live in our memory. They are set in the centre of consciousness, and we then concentrate upon them with the whole life of our soul, with all our power of concentration. Our attention is turned away from everything else, and for a certain space of time which must not be too long, we try to concentrate ourselves upon such a concept, or complex of concepts.

Why must such a concept or complex of concepts be something quite new? When we draw reminiscences out of memory, we can never be quite sure of what takes place within our organism, where processes may lead to certain experiences coming from the unconscious spheres outside the soul. Our cognitive power can only act freely when we confront a sense-perception, for it can be envisaged at any moment and because we are quite sure that a sense-perception is not drawn in some fantastic way out of the reminiscences of our life.

The same applies to that which we now allow to fill our consciousness with the exclusion of all sense-perceptions and to which we yield completely. Though we have no sensory perceptions, we are inwardly just as living as is ordinarily the case with external sense perception. The first thing which should be borne in mind when treading the path to higher knowledge, is that our thinking, which is free from sense impressions, acquires an inner activity which completely claims the attention of our soul, in the same way in which this attention is ordinarily claimed only by an external sense perception. One might say : What we ordinarily experience in connection with an external sense impression, we should learn to experience in connection with that intensified thought-activity which is completely permeated by a clear, conscious will.

This in itself sets up a strong barrier against anything which seeks to enter human consciousness in the form of suggestions, illusions, visions or hallucinations. Spiritual-scientific knowledge, in our meaning of the word, is not understood in the right way if people say : By his exercises, a spiritual investigator might after all be led to hallucinations or to similar results, he may be led into all kinds of pathological conditions of the soul. But those who earnestly consider the way in which Anthroposophy describes the path leading to higher knowledge, will see that this kind of spiritual investigation reveals most clearly of all the true nature of illusions, hallucinations or mediumistic phenomena. It rejects all this severely, as pathological elements ; in fact, the results obtained by real spiritual research, clearly enable us to perceive the worthlessness of such phenomena.

Then one comes to quite a new way of thinking The old way of thinking which is used in ordinary life and in ordinary science, remains. But a new way of thinking is added to it, if we do the exercises principally characterised as thought-exercises (you will find them in my book *Knowledge of the Higher Worlds*, or in my *Outline of an Occult Science*) and if we constantly practise them in a systematic way. (One person will need longer time for the attainment of results, and another person a shorter time). These thoughts, constituting a systematic practice, should be carried out in our consciousness as an inner soul-development.

I might describe this new way of thinking which is added to the old way of thinking in the following way.

Perhaps you will allow me to make a personal remark ; which, however, is not meant personally, but, as you will readily admit, it belongs to the objective part of my descriptions. In the early nineties of the nineteenth century, I wrote my *Philosophy of Spiritual Activity* in order to show that freedom really lives in man's ethical, moral life. There it has its roots. The *Philosophy of Spiritual Activity* called forth many misunderstandings, because people simply cannot penetrate into the way of thinking which is employed in this book.

My *Philosophy of Spiritual Activity* already employs that form of thinking which must be gained by systematic practice in order to reach a knowledge of the higher worlds. It is a first beginning in this direction, a first step which anyone can make in ordinary life. Yet it is at the same time a first step leading to a knowledge of the higher worlds.

Ordinary thinking (it suffices to bear in mind the true nature of the ordinary way of thinking, in order to see that my remarks are justified)—ordinary thinking really consists of spatial perceptions. In our ordinary thinking everything is arranged spatially. Consider that even time is led back to space! For time is expressed by the movements of the clock. The same process in fact is also contained in our physical formulæ. In short, we finally must come to the conclusion that ordinary thinking is a combining way of thinking, one that collects scattered elements. We use this way of thinking in our ordinary sound conditions of life, and in ordinary science.

But the kind of thinking which should be used for the cognition of higher worlds and which is gained with the aid of the exercises I have described, is one which I might call morphological thinking, one in which we think in forms.

This way of thinking is not limited to space; it lives within the medium of time, in the same way in which our ordinary thinking lives within the medium of space. This thinking does not link up one thought with the other; it sets before the soul a kind of thought-organism. When we have a conception, an idea or a thought, we cannot pass over at will to another. Even as in the human organism we cannot pass over at will from the head to any other form, but must first pass over to the neck, then the shoulders, the thorax, etc., even as in an organism everything has a definite structure which must be considered as a *whole*, so the thinking which I characterised as morphological thinking must be inwardly mobile, As stated, it lives within the medium of time, not of space. But it is inwardly so mobile that it produces one form out of another, by constantly growing and producing an organic structure.

It is this morphological way of thinking which should be added to the ordinary way of thinking. It can be attained through exercises of meditation which are described in principle in some of my books. These exercises strengthen and intensify thinking. The morphological way of thinking, the thinking activity which takes its course in forms and pictures, enables us to reach the first stage in the knowledge of super-sensible worlds, namely the stage described in my books as *imaginative knowledge*.

Imaginative knowledge does not as yet supply anything pertaining to an external world. To begin with, it leads only to man's self-knowledge, but it is a far deeper knowledge of self than the one which is ordinarily reached by self-contemplation. This imaginative knowledge brings forms into our consciousness, forms which are experienced just as livingly as any sense-perception. But they have a perculiar quality of their own.

Our ordinary thoughts could not live within our consciousness in a sound way if we were unable to remember them. In regard to spiritual health and a sound development of soul-life, a very great deal depends upon our remembering capacity, upon our memory. Only those who have a continuous memory in their waking-life condition, a memory which goes back to a certain moment in childhood, can be said to be of sound mind.

Perhaps you will also have heard of the terrible condition of certain psychopathic people due to the fact that certain memories are blotted out. Psychiatry knows this state in which memories are blotted out, and it shows us the great importance of a continuous memory if the human soul is to live in a sound condition. This applies to the ordinary development of thought.

But it does not apply to the way of thinking just characterised as morphological or imaginative thinking. When our eye, or some other sense-organ is turned to some external object, the perception can be experienced only as long as our sense-organ is exposed to it. In the same way morphological thinking, or imaginative thinking, only exists while we experience it, and what thus arises within imaginative thinking cannot in the ordinary sense be impressed upon our memory. It must be called forth every time afresh, if it is to be experienced.

Those who reach such an organic-morphological way of thinking which develops as it were into a living process of growth, cannot retain the results of this thinking in their ordinary memory. Freedom, too, can only be characterised by ascending to such growing, constantly developing way of thinking. This is why my *Philosophy of Spiritual Activity* gave rise to so many misunderstandings. But it had to be transmitted through this method of thinking, because freedom is a spiritual experience and it is impossible to come to it with ordinary combining thinking.

Beginners in the method of spiritual science generally think that an imaginative experience can be impressed on the soul like any other thought. But this is not the case. An imaginative thought vanishes from our consciousness. The only thing which can be retained is the *way in which* the imaginative experience was reached. The conditions can be reconstructed, thus giving rise to the experience. If we wish to see again a flower which we have already seen, we must return to it and look at it; in the same way, the inner processes leading to an imaginative experience must be recalled, if we wish to have this experience again.

A spiritual-scientific content cannot be remembered without further ado. This even applies to the most elementary things in honest spiritual-scientific investigation. Here again, allow me to mention something personal, but which is also an objective fact.

You see, what an anthroposophical investigator of spiritual science has to say, cannot, as it were, be transmitted day by day in the form of lectures, in the same way in which natural-scientific facts are generally advanced. Scientific facts can be remembered, they live in our memory and can be set forth with the aid of memory. But the facts which a spiritual-scientific investigator has to advance, must come from his inner living experience. He cannot prepare himself in the same way in which one generally prepares lectures based on memory. The only thing he can do is to recontruct the conditions enabling him to experience the most elementary facts of spiritual science.

We should realise that the spiritual science of Anthroposophy leads in its very first steps to a development of otherwise dormant forces of the human soul, and we should not think that any results can be reached in regard to higher worlds through ordinary philosophical speculations.

The imaginative knowledge described to you just now, leads, as already stated, to a kind of self-knowledge. Finally it leads us to a great tableau in which we simultaneously survey all the organic elements that have built up our whole life from our earthly birth onwards. Inwardly we perceive the creative formative forces which build up the human being and we first perceive them in connection with our own self.

We can see this tableau in the same way in which certain people in danger of death (even natural-scientific thinkers admit this), for instance, when they are drowning, see before them a weaving, living picture of their past life; we do not however, see it as a memory-picture, we do not look upon the small details of life, but we survey its chief facts, the forces which made us progress. We see, as it were, a deeper memory-tableau. At the same time, this tableau does not merely set before us the ordinary thinking life of the soul, but that inner life which works upon the physical organism from the soul.

This conception leads to a standpoint that makes it appear childish that even in the first decades of the 19th century people should have spoken in a speculative way of vital forces, of vitalism. Anthroposophy does not speak of such a vital force. It speaks instead of the conception of life, of what I call the etheric body, or body of formative forces, which represents on the one hand a soul-element, and on the other, a condensed, intensified soul-element which works upon the physical organism.

We are thus led to a deeper knowledge of the soul and also to a deeper knowledge of the way in which the soul-element works within the organism. Let me now give you an example, an elementary but characteristic example:

You know that recognised modern psychology does not go beyond certain speculative ideas in regard to the connections which exist between the soul and the body. The soul is described as if it were the body's motive force, and scientists with a more materialistic mentality consider the body as a plus, which as it were, produces the soul. Most frequently of all modern psychophysicists speak of parallellism, viz., that psychic phenomena and bodily phenomena follow a parallel course, and so forth. But all these things are mere speculations, simply based on the fact that people are unwilling to penetrate with the scientific spirit that prevails elsewhere into the psychical-bodily life of man.

You are all acquainted with the physical concept of latent heat contained in every object, but which does not manifest itself as heat. But this heat can be freed, it is said, if certain conditions are created, and in that case it manifests itself. But before the heat appeared, it existed in the objects as a latent force, where it gives rise to something which does not reveal itself outwardly through heat-processes. We therefore speak of latent heat and of heat which is set free.

This conception—of course, duly modified and extended—should be applied to the soul-life, by observing it in a concrete way, and not speculatively. We can observe the child's growth until the time of its second dentition around the seventh year. Far more than one generally thinks is connected with this second dentition. If we observe the soul-bodily processes in an unprejudiced way, we can see that after the second dentition the child's whole way of thinking, its whole life of representation and feeling, in fact the whole life of the soul, undergoes a complete change.

When the child changes its teeth, it reaches a final point in regard to a certain direction of life. After the second dentition, the human being no longer requires certain forces for the development of his physical organism which he formerly required. The forces which push out (if I may use this trivial expression) the second teeth are not merely localised in the human head, but they are forces which work in the whole body and manifest themselves locally when the second teeth appear. They exist however in the whole physical organism.

Those who observe this whole process as objectively as natural scientists are accustomed to observe and think in natural science, reach the point of recognising that the forces which push out the second teeth were latent forces, bound up with the physical organism. They gave the child's physical body its structure, but with the second dentition they were set free, so that they can now appear in the child as soul-spiritual forces.

Here we may see concretely how the soul-spiritual forces and the bodily organisation are inter-related. This is not seen speculatively, but in a real, concrete way. Those who only wish to observe the soul at one moment and then the body, may speculate or experiment for a long time, yet they will only come to quite abstract results in regard to the connnection which exists between the soul and the body. But those who observe the processes in the sequence of time, will find that after the second dentition certain soul-forces appear in the child revealing a more sharply outlined concept of memory, more sharply outlined feelings, and they will know that these are forces in the soul which were set free and which now manifest, whereas formerly they were submerged in the physical organism. Observations, not mere speculative thought, shows them the connection between the body and the soul.

This example shows us how we should investigate the inter-activity of soul and body with the aid of imaginative thought. We gain insight into the activity of the soul-spiritual forces in the physical-bodily organisation. This is what is presented in the tableau which I have described.

If we have reached the point of developing this imaginative way of thinking, we must proceed further with the strength thus gained. Even as a muscle grows stronger through practice, so the thinking power grows stronger if we do these exercises which are described in greater detail in the books mentioned. If we develop within us an intensified thinking endowed with plastic forces which lives in time, other forces of our soul may be developed and intensified.

The ordinary thoughts of life come and go, or we try to get rid of them either by discarding them from our soul, or the organism sees to it that we forget them, and so forth. But the thoughts of the kind described, which are called up in our consciousness for the sake of gaining higher knowledge, cannot be blotted out as easily as ordinary thoughts. A great effort must be made to forget them. This is a second kind of exercise: an artificial forgetting, as it were, an artificial suppression of thought.

If we have practised this artificial suppression of thought for a sufficiently long time, corresponding to our individual development and predispositions, we become able to suppress the whole tableau of which I have spoken, so that our consciousness is quite empty. The only thing which should remain to us is our calm thinking power, permeated by the will. But this thinking now appears in a new form.

I have now described to you two ways of thinking: the ordinary way of thinking which is connected with space, and a way of thinking which has a growth of its own, in which one thought always grows out of the other, even as in a living organism one limb is connected with the other.

If this morphological way of thinking is practised for a certain time, we gradually develop a third way of thinking, which we need in order to ascend to a higher stage of supersensible knowledge. We need this kind of thinking when we rise to a stage which is higher than that in which we merely survey our own organisation.

Imaginative knowledge leads us to a survey of our own organisation, so that we say to ourselves: Here on earth, the soul-spiritual element, which is supersensible, works upon the physical body. We must use this morphological way of thinking, for otherwise it is not possible to understand what takes place in the medium of time and works upon the physical body out of a supersensible sphere, for this is something which undergoes continual metamorphoses. Our thinking must become mobile and our thoughts must be inwardly connected with each other. Mere combining thought cannot grasp the life which proceeds from the spirit, this can only be grasped by an inwardly living thinking.

But still another way of thinking must be developed if we wish to rise up to the next stage of supersensible knowledge. Let me use an example in order to explain this to you. Even this example is difficult to penetrate, but I think you will be able to grasp what I mean.

Let us bear in mind the fact that Goethe tried to interpret the single cranial bones as metamorphoses of the vertebræ. In the single bones of the skull Goethe perceived transformations of the vertebræ. Though somewhat modified, modern science also adopts this view, but it is no longer entirely in keeping with Goethe's conception; nevertheless this view is valid to-day.

It does not suffice, however, to consider the purely morphological derivation of the cranial bones. We must go further if we wish to understand the relationship of the human head to the remaining human organism (we will restrict ourselves to the skeleton). We must not only envisage a transformation, but something very different. Let us ask, for instance: What relation exists between the bony system of the arms or legs and the bony system of the cranial bones, of the bones of the head? Here it is the case that the metamorphoses through which one form gives rise to the other can only be grasped if we bear in mind that this is not only a spatial metamohrposis taking place within the medium of time, but that quite another process takes place which is very difficult to understand, namely, a kind of turning over, a reversal.

If you wish to grasp the mutual relation between the bones of the leg and the bones of the skull, you must compare the external surface of the skull with the inner surface of a hollow bone, let us say of the upper thigh bone. This means that the inner side of the thigh bone must be turned inside out, so that also its elasticity would change; its inner surface would in that case be turned outwards and correspond to the external surface of a cranial bone; and vice versa, the outer surface of the thigh bone would not correspond to the outer surface of the cranium, but to its inner surface.

Imagine this process of metamorphosis like a glove which is turned inside out, but at the same time the elasticity of the glove undergoes a change. A new form arises. It is as if the glove is not only turned inside out, but takes on quite a different shape through the new elasticity.

You see, as a first indication of this third kind of thinking I must bring before you a very complicated process. This kind of thinking does not only live in constantly changing forms, but it is able to reverse the inner structure, so as to change its form.

This can only be achieved through the fact that now our thinking no longer lives in the medium of time, for in this process of reversion the subject of our thoughts transcends space and time and penetrates into a reality which lies beyond space and time.

I know that we cannot immediately become familiar with this third kind of thinking, which differs so greatly from the combining and the the plastic ways of thinking. It is not easy to penetrate into this third kind of thinking, which dives down, as it were, into spacelessness and timelessness; it is not easy to understand that it reappears in a changed form turned inside out.

Anthroposophy does not wish to speak of the higher worlds in the amateurish way adopted by so many people, but because Anthroposophy is as honest as any other honest science it must point out that it is not only necessary to abandon the sphere of higher science, but that it is even necessary to acquire a completely new way of thinking.

If we wish to advance to a qualitative thinking man's inner forces must be held together in an entirely different way, for the whole quality of our thinking undergoes a change during this process of reversal, when the inner is turned into the outer.

When we succeed in submerging our thought into a qualitative element, it is possible to ascend to that stage of knowledge of the supersensible worlds which follows the stage of imaginative thought.

If the tableau of which I have spoken has been suppressed, so that an empty consciousness is established, then we have an empty consciousness for a certain time; this can be achieved if we suppress merely a concept. But when such a reality is suppressed, when we suppress forces which are constantly at the service of growth and nutrition during our earthly existence, we dive down into a completely new world. We then really are in the higher worlds and the ordinary physical world lies behind us like a memory. We must have it as a memory, for otherwise we should not be of sound mind; without memory we should be psychopaths, subjected to hallucinations and to illusions.

If we proceed in the right way along the path of spiritual investigation, we maintain our calm thoughtful consciousness permeated by the will even when we ascend to the highest worlds and there can be no question of falling a prey to hallucinations or suggestions.

When we are subjected to hallucinations or suggestions, the ordinary consciousness is entirely supplanted by a pathological consciousness. In the state of consciousness which Anthroposophy strives to reach for the attainment of knowledge of higher worlds, the essential thing is to maintain our ordinary consciousness in its full extent, so that we keep our sound common sense and our calm state of mind while ascending to the higher worlds. Even the thinking strengthened with the reversion of thought already mentioned, or the super-morphological thought, even this exists only for the sake of penetrating in full consciousness into the higher worlds. We then really experience the higher worlds and their spiritual contents.

Through the imaginative consciousness which enables us to gain a conception of the forces working in us from birth onwards, a conception of supersensible forces working upon the physical body, we gain knowledge of that part of our being which existed *before* our birth, or before we were conceived within the physical world, when we still lived in a soul-spiritual world surrounded by soul-spiritual beings, even as here on earth, during the time between birth and death, we are surrounded by physical beings.

In short, we experience the eternal kernel of man's being, when we look behind birth into that stage of existence through which we passed before the earth received us into the physical stream of heredity; we experience man's eternal being in his spiritual environment.

Thus it is neither speculation, nor a system of thought that has led us to a knowledge of the higher worlds; it is a beholding. Even as the development of the body, from the embryonic stage onwards, gives us a conception of the external physical world, so the steps described to you in principle (details can be found in the books I have mentioned) lead us to a knowledge of soul-processes and enable us to live in a spiritual world in which we existed before birth and into which we enter when we pass through the portal of death. Objective vision leads to a knowledge of the higher worlds.

I have now described to you in the first place a path of knowledge. But this is incompletely described if it is merely described as a path of knowledge, for the experiences which we gain call for something besides a mere activity of thought. Though it may be difficult to acquire these two higher forms of thinking, there is something else which presents far greater difficulties.

If here in the physical world we preferably cling to observation and experiments, it is because in a certain way this sets our mind at rest in regard to the reality of our knowledge. From the standpoint of a theory of knowledge one may dispute about the true nature of sense-perceptions and their relation to reality, etc., but this is not the point just now; the point is that sense-perception gives us a guarantee for the truth of our soul's experience, the reflected images of our sense-perceptions which arise in the soul; we set our minds at rest by leaning upon the external reality.

The disease of spiritism has arisen in recent times; which in just such a way seeks to establish the reality of the spiritual by external observation.

One cannot of course be a stronger materialist than by being a spiritist. Spiritism is but the enhanced form of materialism, for in spiritism people not only wish to establish the reality of physical substance, which they perhaps consider as the only reality, but they even wish to show that the spirit appears in the same form as matter, i.e. that the spirit itself is nothing but matter. What arises in the form of spiritism is the last phase of materialism and draws out of it the last consequences.*

Real spiritual science seeks for an ascent into the spiritual worlds and not a drawing down of the spiritual worlds into material processes.

But when we ascend to the spiritual world in the manner described we no longer have the support which the external world provides, as it were, for our soul-experiences. We need something which gives the certainty that we are not floating in emptiness, that our soul-experiences in the higher worlds are not mere fancies; we need a support in the same way in which the external sense perceptions give us a support in our ordinary life. This again can only be reached through the development of inner forces.

Please do not misunderstand me. I do not mean that the forces which we already have in ordinary life (one has to speak in terms taken from ordinary life) suffice. We must develop forces even in spheres which are not the spheres of thought, in order to reach not only vision, but vision rooted in reality.

---

* See Rudolf Steiner: "Geschichte des Spiritismus" and "Geschichte des Hypnotismus und Sonnambulismus."

The assurance which our sense-perceptions provide from outside, consists in the fact that one sense supports the other. When we have an impression of sound or of sight, we do not immediately know whether this is a hallucination or not. We can only be sure of the impression gained, when we are supported—I might say—by the sense of gravitation, when another sense comes to our aid, when an impression which is not sufficiently guaranteed by the sense of sight or hearing can be supported by some other sense.

What is it that gives us the right to speak of reality in the physical world? Several things may be taken into consideration. I should have to speak for hours from the standpoint of a theory of knowledge (of course, I cannot do this now) in order to prove the fact which I now briefly wish to summarize. But if you follow the corresponding train of thought you will see that the following fact can be accepted: In the physical world we designate a fact as " real " when it influences us in such a way that we should be obliged to deny our own existence were we to deny the existence of that thing. If you not only hear the sound of a bell, but if you can touch it and discover its connection with other things, you would have to blot out your own self if you were not able to say that the external object is real, when you experience its reality within your soul. An external object can be called real, if we should have to deny our own reality in denying the reality of the object.

What we describe as reality is therefore intimately related with our own reality. That is why forces must also be drawn out of our own reality, which is a soul-spiritual reality, and these moral forces may be compared with an object which I grasp and which shows itself to be heavy. Within our own being we must seek supporting forces for the reality of the spiritual worlds into which we penetrate in the way I have described.

This can only be done if we develop certain moral qualities which we already have in our ordinary ethical attitude in life ; the moral forces must be strengthened in the same way in which we strengthen the force of thought. These moral forces should not only be developed for the sake of our ethical life, they must be further strengthened.

Let me now speak to you only of two kinds. The first is what we call moral courage, or courage in general ; this should be intensified in the same way in which the forces of thinking are intensified. The forces of courage within us may be intensified if the retrospective tableau arising through imagination is placed before the soul and we then look upon it and experience it in the right way. We then discover a higher kind of courage in our own life ; when diving down into this tableau we discover inner forces of courage which are greater than those which we generally use in our external life, which is more or less passive. This courage should be intensified.

There is another moral force which should be intensified. Whereas courage is generally connected with the life of feeling and resembles an inner sense of sureness, a certain inner power, it is necessary to unfold certain forces which are connected with the will and which consist, for example, in the fact that at certain given moments we determine to do something, which we set about to do at some later time, by establishing with an iron will the conditions which enable us to carry out our resolution. An Anthroposophical spiritual investigator should carry out these exercises quite systematically. He should inwardly connect his present will-impulses with impulses that were in him at a former time.

In our ordinary life we give ourselves up to the present. But in the life which is to bring us into higher worlds we must visualise with an inner continuity of the will. Throughout many years we should be able to hold a purpose in mind and carry out at some later time things which we once resolved to do. This unfolds strong forces which support the will; it develops a strong current of volition which we ourselves establish within us.

This a special form of self-discipline. We are then no longer dependent on external circumstances or on ideals which induce us to do certain things, but by the will-impulse we inwardly connect in a soul-spiritual manner a later moment of our soul-life with an earlier moment. If a higher form of courage unfolds within our soul, if we develop the continuity of our will-impulses so that our will-impulses endure over the gulfs of time then we come to the point of ascending into the higher worlds, we shall be able to verify the reality of what we then perceive in the same way in which we do this in regard to the external physical world. The reality which we perceive there must be verified with the aid of inwardly intensified forces.

Hence the path leading to the spiritual worlds is not the development of a one-sided cognitive force, but the development of the whole human being in the direction of thinking, feeling and will, which implies a striving after knowledge, an æsthetic striving and an ethical striving. This path leading to the higher worlds is at the same time a religious immersion, a religious deepening of the human being.

There is one essential point which should be borne in mind : In modern times, even as through science to a great extent doubts have arisen in regard to the spiritual worlds, so through science these spiritual worlds must be conquered again. It is shortsighted to believe that the religious life must suffer through the fact that it is possible to ascend to the spiritual worlds with the same clear consciousness that we have in the physical world.

Those who advance criticism in this respect, generally do so because they think that the spiritual science of Anthroposophy remains within the limits of the intellect and rationalism. This is not the case. The whole human being, with his feeling and his will, flows into the development of thought, which is acquired in the manner I have described. The path leading to higher worlds indicated by the spiritual science of Anthroposophy is the unfolding and the development of the whole human being. Even as in ordinary physical life thinking grows out of the organism like a flower, so higher knowledge grows out of the fully developed human being, who unfolds all his forces harmoniously and intensively along the path leading to the higher worlds.

Through the development of mere thinking we only come to a world of images. If reality is to be perceived within this world of images, we must develop in the way I have indicated the courage contained in moral forces, the will contained in our character, our own individual will which we maintain throughout periods of time.

These two forces, and others, which you will find described in the books already mentioned before, should be intensified. The human being as a whole must be led in a soul-spiritual way into those other worlds in which he lives before he is conceived by physical forces and enters physical life on earth or in which he lives after passing through the portal of death.

If we wish to ascend to this life with knowledge, if we wish to acquire the vision of the supersensible worlds, the *whole* soul-spiritual being of man must be led towards them—not only some vague part of him which desires to become acquainted with these worlds theoretically.

The spiritual science of Anthroposophy can therefore fructify the whole life of man. Anthroposophy does not seek in some abstruse mystical way to estrange us from the world, but strives on the contrary to lead us into practical life, into a life which is truly practical. That is why it can be so fruitful for science and art, social and religious life—in short, for the most different spheres of life.

I can only give a few indications in this connection.

If we can see the life-tableau of retrospective vision of which I have spoken, a tableau which is in reality a structure of formative forces moving in the stream of time, if we can recognise this structure, we can also see how the human body arises out of this system of forces and how it develops. For it is only an external illusion to speak of the heart, the lungs, etc. ; in reality, the heart is a process, and the external spatial form of the heart is merely the process which is held fast for a time. This applies to every organ. What is retained for a moment within a certain shape, can be perceived. But we cannot perceive the incessant life-process giving rise to health and illness unless we attain to a knowledge of the supersensible formative forces of the body.

Medicine, and therapy in particular, can be essentially fructified by spiritual science, and we have already opened Clinical-therapeutic Institutes in Stuttgart and Dornach where the sickness of humanity can benefit from knowledge derived from Anthroposophy.

Spiritual science can fructify life in many other directions. When a School for Spiritual Science was opened at Dornach it was not possible to give it any ordinary kind of frame. What the friends of our anthroposophical world-conception had in mind when they wished to erect a building for a school of spiritual science was something quite special. Let me explain this by a comparison.

Take a nut with its shell. An unprejudiced person will think that the nut's shell must have the form which it has, because the nut itself has a definite form. The shell forms part of the nut. When a spiritual world-conception, such as that contained in the Anthroposophical movment, is called into life, the members may find themselves in the position to erect a building and they may think : Let us go to an architect who will draw us a plan in this or in that style, in accordance with traditional customs, or something thought out which would not in any way be connected with the things which are to be cultivated within it—just as if the nut's shell were not to fit the nut !

Since Anthroposophy is not a mere theory, and does not merely live in words, the Anthroposophical Movement can therefore not proceed in this way, not even in regard to its frame. At Dornach, the words which resound from the speaker's platform, the scenes on the stage, whatever art is presented through word or movement from the stage, must have exactly the same inner essential style as that which is expressed in the walls, in the external architecture of the Building. Even as the *shell* of the nut is formed by the same forces which formed the nut, so the Anthroposophical realities which come to expresssion in the world must have an artistic frame and call into being a new style of architecture.

It was therefore an organic necessity for a new style of architecture to arise in Dornach. This new style is simply the externally visible part of the reality which lives soul-spiritually in the world. One will be able to see what is the intention of Anthroposophy to-day just through the fructifying influence which it exercises also upon the artistic spheres of life.

In Eurhythmy, which is only a beginning, we called into life a human art of movement in which the single artists or the groups of artists do not dance or pantomime, but in which the forms of movement constitute a speech based on laws just as strict as those of spoken language, or a visible song, similar to that which one ordinarily hears in the form of sound. Eurhythmy is entirely drawn out of the law of man, in spirit, soul and body.

Through Anthroposophy we have thus been able to exercise a fructifying influence on many different spheres of art.

In my *Threefold State* the attempt has been made to face the great social problems of the present time from the anthroposophical standpoint. Those who bear in mind that from the anthroposophical standpoint the whole human being has to be taken into account in the social question, and not only that part which is accessible to a rationalistic science, to Marxism and similar directions of thought, must admit that forces which penetrate into the higher spiritual worlds can also penetrate into the social laws of human life, for these in fact are soul-spiritual laws pertaining to the higher worlds; they can also lead us to laws which are able to call into existence satisfactory social conditions in human life. For it is a spiritual element which unites human beings in their life in common, and physical links are simply formed out of the spiritual.

The terrible catastrophe of the present time and the decadent forces which now hold sway are largely due to the fact that people forget this spiritual foundation. Humanity must again permeate itself with the spirit.

Anthroposophy has also had a fructifying influence on education, pedagogy. At the Waldorf School at Stuttgart, founded by Emil Molt, the results of anthroposophical research in the direction of a true knowledge of man are applied to the developing human being, to the child. The paths which lead us to the higher worlds also enable us to observe the child year by year and week by week, as it develops from birth to puberty; it enables us to see in the child the forces which it brought with it from the spiritual worlds and which the teacher or the educator must conjure forth.

I can only give a few indications in this direction, for at the Waldorf School we have tried to develop all these things in detail into an art of education. These are a few examples showing how Anthroposophy can influence different spheres of life.

I already told you that Anthroposophy can also fructify religious life, because it leads in a scientific way to the higher worlds and because it shows us the true nature of man's eternal being which he bears in his transient earthly existence as an ever-developing spiritual element not accessible to the ordinary forces of cognition. It shows this eternal essence in its own element, in the supersensible worlds. Higher vision can discover it there. Here it is concealed, because when it enters earthly life through birth it becomes absorbed by the physical form. But this fact does not deprive the spirit of its living forces, for the physical substance only conceals it. The spiritual can however be perceived in physical substance, in matter. An aid to such an insight is provided by the paths leading to the supersensible worlds, which Anthroposophy seeks to indicate.

Anthroposophy does not wish on this account to lead us away from the ordinary world into asceticism, but it opens out the paths to the spirit, to the supersensible worlds in such a way that with the aid of the spirit we can once more form and shape material, practical life.

The essential thing is to recognise a creative power in the spirit. The spiritual world would be weak indeed were we to experience it only as an uncreative element transcending matter. There are many people who say: The physical aspect of the world is something low, let us rise above it; let us abandon matter in order to reach high spiritual spheres.

Many things assuredly must be overcome in order to attain a knowledge of this spirit, but when we have reached it through love (and it can only be reached through love, through religious devotion and warmth, for the development of the moral capacities mentioned above lead us, through love, into the supersensible worlds) then we take hold of the spiritual, supersensible essence as we approach matter. For the strong spiritual element is not one which flees matter, but one which forms matter, which can be spiritually active within matter. This is one aspect.

On the other hand let me tell you one other thing which should be borne in mind, my dear fellow-students, namely that the spiritual science of Anthroposophy, as it is meant here, treads the paths leading to the supersensible worlds in such a way that the results obtained along these paths do not stand outside the ordinary natural-scientific facts and their operations, but penetrate them as a soul-spiritual force.

Even as a person is a full human being in the true meaning of the word because here on earth he lives in a physical body which bears within it a soul-spiritual element, so science can only be science in the full meaning of the word if it is not a mere knowledge of the external, physical reality, but if this knowledge can be permeated by the knowledge of the spiritual worlds. For this reason the spiritual science of Anthroposophy wishes to set itself within the other science by meeting the demands of the being and nature both of man and of the universe. Even as in his physical life man must bear within him spirit and soul, so a real spiritual science which opens up true reliable ways into the supersensible spiritual worlds, must become the spirit and soul of ordinary science dealing with the physical world. And even as the spirit and the soul in man do not fight or rebel against the body, but should harmonise with it fully, so the spiritual science of Anthroposophy should be in full harmony with real, genuine knowledge of nature and history.

THE FOUNDATIONS OF SPIRITUAL SCIENCE

I wish to give you in three lectures a survey of what Anthroposophy has to say concerning the Human Being and his relation to the Universe. The universe and man are undoubtedly the two most important problems, for they embrace every question dealing with science and life, every problem of greatest and smallest importance.

It lies in the nature of these problems that in regard to these things I must limit myself to the anthroposophical horizon, that is to say, to the things connected with the great life-problems of human existence which transcend the knowledge gained through sensory perception and which lie beyond the sphere of ordinary science.

In regard to the human being, self-knowledge is undoubtedly a problem which must appeal to us most of all. For in order to gain a foundation and a firm standpoint in life, we must first obtain a conception of our own nature. And it must be said that at all times people have sought to gain a knowledge of the universe, for they knew that the mysteries of the world's evolution are connected with man's own being; they knew that they could only learn something about man's being by seeking to know what the universe is able to give them, the universe of which the human being forms part.

Moreover, it cannot be denied that in connection with a knowledge of man and of the universe modern people show a deep interest for everything which transcends ordinary science, and we may say that innumerable attempts are now being made to transcend the spheres of ordinary science in order to investigate what lies beyond birth and death, beyond the world which can be fathomed by ordinary sense-perception and by the understanding which is based upon it.

In recent times we can observe above all that there are scientific investigators who in many ways endeavour to transcend the spheres indicated above, and as an introduction let me mention a few striking conceptions of modern investigators, examples which prove that the keen interest in the problems which will form the subject of my three lectures really exists, but which prove at the same time how very difficult it is, even in the case of people well grounded in science, to penetrate into the sphere of the soul and of the spirit. As I do not wish to speak in abstract terms, let me proceed immediately from concrete examples.

A German scientist who worked very hard to discover how to penetrate into the supersensible nature of the soul, and how to investigate the influence exercised by the soul's supersensible nature upon the body's physical nature, tried to give many examples taken from his medical and scientific experience, showing the soul's influence, the influence of an unquestionably psychic essence upon the body. A marked example contained in one of the books written by this physician and scientist named Schleich, who was personally well known to me, is the following. He describes a patient, who came to him in a great state of excitement, because in the office he had pricked his skin with an inky nib. The doctor could ascertain that it was quite an insignificant scratch. But the patient was under the delusion that this prick with an inky nib had given him a blood poisoning and that he would have to die unless his hand was amputated, and he begged the doctor to amputate his hand, his arm as quickly as possible.

The doctor could only tell him to be calm, that he would be quite well again in a couple of days and that there was nothing to be afraid of. As a responsible doctor he had to tell him this and could not, of course, amputate his arm.

But the patient was not satisfied. He went to another doctor who told him exactly the same thing and also refused to amputate his arm. Schleich was nevertheless nervous, for he was acquainted with soul-moods, and so he enquired the next day how the patient was feeling and he was told that the man had died.

The autopsy did not reveal any trace of blood-poisoning, or similiar symptoms. This was out of the question. Yet the patient had died.

In connection with this case, Schleich remarks : Death caused by radical auto-suggestion.

The patient had the fixed idea that he had to die; it was an extremely radical auto-suggestion and he really did die under its influence.

This is the statement of an investigator well acquainted with all the natural-scientific methods, with all the medical methods. He reports this case in order to show a purely psychical influence, i.e. the influence of a thought, upon bodily processes, an influence showing, according to Schleich, that death set in as a result.

Schleich mentions many other cases, less marked and radical, in order to prove that it is possible to observe the soul, living in thoughts, feelings, sensations and will-impulses, and that the soul can really influence the body. He wishes to describe, as it were, the influence of the supersensible upon the physical.

Another case is described by a far more conspicuous scientist, by Sir Oliver Lodge. Sir Oliver Lodge lost his son Raymond in the last war. He fell on the Belgian-German frontier, and Oliver Lodge, who had long ago felt the inclination to build a bridge leading from the sensory-natural-scientific sphere to the supersensible sphere, was deeply stirred by the loss of his beloved son. Through many incidents, which are not directly connected with this matter and which I need not relate, he was induced to use the mediumistic power of a certain person, in order to enter into connection with the departed soul of his son, Raymond.

When such a case arises in ordinary spiritistic circles, it is not necessary to consider it seriously, for one knows how unscientific these meetings are, and how amateurishly and unscientifically such cases are judged and investigated in them. But the matter must be taken more seriously when we have to do with one of the greatest of modern scientists, with a man so thoroughly at home in the sphere of external, natural scientific research and so well acquainted with scientific methods. That is why Oliver Lodge's book on his spiritual intercourse with his son Raymond, made such a deep impression on the world.

On reading this book, we immediately feel that it is written by a man who does not approach the investigation of such things superficially, but by a conscientious and responsible scientist. Even in other things, which I will not mention here, one can see that Oliver Lodge applies to this sphere the same way of thinking, the same scientific method which he is accustomed to apply in his physical laboratory. The real facts which he relates, and which, one might say, rightly produced such a deep impression upon all those who read Sir Oliver Lodge's book, are as follows :

Through the medium in question, Oliver Lodge and a few other people who were present at the séances, were told that his son, that is, the soul, the spirit of Oliver Lodge's son, wished to describe a scene enacted on the Belgian-German frontier shortly before his death, and the medium related that Raymond Lodge had a photograph taken and described this act in detail. It was expressly stated that two photographs were taken; these two photographs were carefully described and attention was drawn to the fact that upon the second photograph Sir Oliver Lodge's son had a somewhat different pose from that on the first one.

When these communications were made in London through the medium (Sir Oliver Lodge describes it so that one can really see—I emphasize this expressly—that he took every possible scientific precaution), at the time when these experiments were made, no one in London knew anything about these photographs, nor that they had been taken. After examining all the facts, Sir Oliver Lodge came to the conclusion that if this message were true, it could only come from his son, from the departed son himself.

In fact, after two or three weeks, the photographs which no one had seen before really arrived in London. They corresponded with the description given by the medium, or, as Sir Oliver Lodge believed, with the description given by the soul of his son. Even a scientist could see in this fact, to begin with, one might say, "*experimentum crucis.*" Nobody in London could possibly have seen the photographs. It appeared that the description was correct even in regard to the fact that two photographs were taken and that the second one shows a difference. The photographer had taken the photograph of the group which included Raymond Lodge twice, and for the second photograph he had shifted his camera a little. All this had been described exactly. A conscientious scientist could not find the slightest reason for questioning the medium's communication.

The two radical cases I have described to you, show that the longing, the great desire of unquestionably serious modern scientists lead them to seek a knowledge which goes beyond the facts revealed by ordinary external scientific research.

But one who speaks of the foundations of anthroposophical research, one who speaks from an anthroposophical standpoint, must draw attention to the fact that the methods of this investigation differ from those adopted even by such serious minded scientists. For, in regard to a scientific way of thinking and a scientific mentality the foundations of anthroposophical research (I hope that my three lectures will make things clear to you from every aspect) should be stricter and more conscientious than any other, even in comparison with such strict scientists as the above. And one who ventures to criticize such great scientists is perhaps first called upon to judge and to explain the far greater certainty constituting the foundation of Anthroposophy, which is so often accused of advancing fantastic notions; this certainty given by Anthroposophy is far greater than that transmitted by the most conscientious scientific investigators of the present time. In order to indicate the critical attitude, the earnest and truly scientific character of Anthroposophy and its foundations, let me first bring forward the critical objections which can be raised against the scientific interpretations given in the two above mentioned examples.

Let me now begin with these things, for in connection with to-day's subject my last two lectures already contained many (*) explanations, so that the essential facts are known to the great majority of those who are now present; allow me therefore briefly to illumine the things already explained to you from another angle.

The following objection must be raised in regard to Schleich and his case of " death through auto-suggestion." Please accept this, to begin with, as a simple critical objection showing how matters might also be viewed! Let us suppose that the man who pricked his hand with an inky nib and who believed that he had blood poisoning, really had some unknown inner defect, so that sudden death through a natural cause would have arisen in any case during the night after the accident. Such cases of sudden death really exist. On the other hand, all those who seriously investigate what can be achieved by a strengthening and intensification of the human cognitive powers, in the direction which I tried to indicate during the last few days, know that certain undefined soul-forces may be driven to a special climax through some abnormal conditions, through—one can really say—abnormal pathological conditions. Such cases undoubtedly exist and are critically described in books, so that everyone can test them, whenever the human will (and we shall see how this is possible) becomes transformed and thus attains cognitive power. Since the human will is directed towards the

---

* 25th November. *The Reality of the Higher Worlds.* 26th November. *Paths to the Knowledge of Higher Worlds.*

future, it is able, under certain pathological conditions, to have a premonition of events which prepare themselves, of events which will take place in the future out of the whole connections of a person's life. It is a matter of indifference whether we call this a foreboding, or whether we give it any other name. But it is a fact that under certain pathological conditions of a lighter nature, which do not clearly appear in the form of illness, a person may foresee, in the form of a picture, that he will, for instance, in fourteen days be thrown from his horse. All precautions will be useless, for he cannot perceive the accompanying circumstances. He has simply had a foreboding, he has simply foreseen an event about to take place.

The critical objection which must be raised by one who really knows the spiritual connections of man in a deeper sense, is that in the case of Schleich's patient, the factors which brought about his sudden death on the following night, can simply have already existed and that he had had an inner presentiment of his approaching death. Such a presentiment need not be fully conscious; it can quite well remain in the subconscious depths of the soul. But its influence upon consciousness manifests itself in symptoms which can be designated as nervousness and restlessness. One does all manner of unpremeditated things, and it is quite possible to prick one's finger with an inky nib under the influence of the nervousness arising from such a premonition. The person in question therefore simply knew unconsciously (let me use this paradoxical expression) that he would die. He did not clothe this in the statement that he had a presentiment of his death, but he grew nervous, pricked his hand with the nib and clung to the belief that he would have to die through blood poisoning. Thus it was not a case of death through auto-suggestion, but the man in question had had a presentiment of his coming death and all his actions were determined by this. In that case Schleich simply mistakes cause and effect, there is no auto-suggestion, as Schleich supposes, to the effect that a conscious thought exercised so strong a suggestion that death ensued; but death would have arisen in any case and the death-presentiment was the cause of the patient's fixed idea.

You see, even such things can be viewed critically, if another, undoubtedly possible thing is borne in mind; namely, that certain subconscious conditions which always exist in the soul, faintly rise to the surface of ordinary consciousness, but masked. In the unconscious depths of the human soul many conscious manifestations have quite a different aspect, and ordinary consciousness simply gives them a different interpretation.

Let us now turn to the other case, that of Sir Oliver Lodge. Undoubtedly you are all acquainted with the phenomenon known as "second sight." Through an intensification of the human cognitive forces, it is possible to perceive things which cannot be perceived by the ordinary sound senses; it is possible, as it were, to see things in a way which is not in keeping with the ordinary conditions of environing space, so that this perceptive faculty can, so to speak, transcend space and time. This fact supplies the critical objection which must be raised even against the conscientiousness of an Oliver Lodge. For Sir Oliver Lodge uses this *experimentum crucis* in order to prove that his son's soul and none other must have spoken to him from the Beyond. But those who know the fine and intimate way in which second sight works, and that under certain abnormal conditions the intimate character of such a perceptive capacity is really able to overcome space and time (mediums always possess this perceptive faculty, though in the great majority of cases this is not to their advantage) those who are acquainted with this fact, also know that a person endowed with second sight can go to the point of giving a description as in the case of Sir Oliver Lodge's son, a description which may be characterised as follows :—

The two photographs arrived in London two or three weeks after the séance. The attention of the people who were present at the séance was turned towards these pictures, that is to something pertaining to the future. And this fact pertaining to the future could be interpreted by a kind of second sight which the medium possessed.

In that case, it can no longer be said that Raymond Lodge's soul shone supersensibly into the room where Sir Oliver Lodge was making his experiments. Here, we simply have to do with something enacted completely upon the physical plane, that is to say, with a vision of the future surpassing the ordinary perceptive capacity, but which does not justify the belief that a soul from beyond the threshold manifested itself in the séance room.

I mention these two examples and the objections against them, in order to awaken in you a feeling for the conscientiousness and for the critical attitude of anthroposophical spiritual research. The spiritual investigation practised in Anthroposophy does not at first proceed from any abnormal phenomena (the two last lectures proved this), but from completely normal conditions of human life, which appear in the forces of cognition, of the will and of feeling. Anthroposophical research seeks to develop these forces which enable one to gain a knowledge of the supersensible worlds, in order to be, as it were, inwardly entitled to this knowledge, and in order to gain the true conscientiousness required in a training which strengthens thought.

Meditation exercises, such as those recently described to you, strengthen our thought to a high degree, so that our way of thinking becomes just as alive and intensive as sensory perception. Then there are the will exercises which I have already mentioned to you, and which will be characterised more fully in these lectures. Will-exercises require above all an intensive observation of normal life, we must become quite familiar with the conditions in which we **normally live.**

A short time ago, a scientist published a brief résumé of the science of Anthroposophy inaugurated by me. This man is in no way a blind believer. He briefly recapitulates what I have been giving you as Anthroposophy, a material which already constitutes a voluminous literature. He recapitulates it, at the same time declaring that he is neither for nor against Anthroposophy, but then he makes a remark which has the semblance of being that of a strong opponent, although the author is neither an opponent nor a follower. I must confess that this cutting remark pleased me exceedingly, particularly if seen in the light in which Anthroposophy appears in comparison with the rest of modern culture. The writer remarks that in the light of ordinary consciousness many of my statements produce an irresistibly comical effect. I must admit that I like this remark for the following simple reason : When things are mentioned, such as Sir Oliver Lodge's case, or the other case reported by me, people prick up their ears, because in a certain way this appeals to their sensationalism and because it differs from what they are accustomed to hear.

This does not seem irresistibly comical to them. But when an Anthroposophist is obliged to establish a connection with altogether normal and human things, with human memory, or with the ordinary expressions of the human will, and explains that through certain exercises human thought may be intensified and that through self-education the will can be developed so that one changes and is able to penetrate as a transformed human being into the supersensible world—and because he uses ordinary words designating things which ordinarily surround us, words which people do not like to apply to anything else—then he may produce an " irresistibly comical effect." Many things therefore have such an irresistibly comical effect on people who only wish to apply the words to things to which they are applied in ordinary life. To an anthroposophical spiritual investigator, such views on Anthroposophy frequently appear like a letter which some one is supposed to read, but instead of reading it begins to make a chemical analysis of the ink with which it is written. I must confess that many statements on Anthroposophy really appear to me as if a person were to analyse the ink used in writing a letter, instead of reading it.

The essential point in the foundations of Anthroposophy is that one starts from completely normal human experiences, that one has a good knowledge of modern scientific truths, of modern ethical life, and develops these very things more intensively, so that one can penetrate into the higher worlds through an intensification of the cognitive forces which already exist less intensely in ordinary life and in science. One must of course have an understanding for these ordinary human experiences. One must pay attention to thoroughly ordinary normal experiences, which, however, we are not very much interested in observing carefully. Things must, so to speak, become enigmas and problems. Although they form part of ordinary life, one easily fails to see their enigmatic character. And here already begins for many people the "irresistibly comical effect," that is, when one begins to say: The questions connected with man's alternating conditions of waking and sleeping must above all be looked upon as enigmas.

During our life, we continually change over from the condition of waking to that of sleeping, but we do not take much notice of this pendulum of life, swaying between the conditions of waking and sleeping. The strangest theories have been advanced in this connection. I might talk for a long time, were I to mention some of these theories relating to the alternating conditions of waking and sleeping. But let me mention only one, the most well-known and usual one, namely that one simply takes for granted that when the human being is awake he gets tired and when he is sufficiently tired goes to sleep, and that sleep in its turn counter-balances fatigue. Sleep (this can be described in one or the other way, more or less materialistically) eliminates the causes of fatigue.

I should like to know if radical supporters of this theory can really say that fatigue is the cause of sleep, when for instance, they observe a person who really has no cause whatever for getting tired during the day—let us say, a fat gentleman living on private means, who goes to a more or less solid concert or to a lecture, not late in the evening, but in the afternoon, and who falls asleep not after the first five minutes, but after two minutes!

These things at first may really present a slightly comical aspect, but if they are viewed from every side, their earnest enigmatic character must stand before our soul. Those who believe that the alternating conditions of waking and sleeping can be studied with the aid of the ordinary scientific methods applied to-day, will never reach a satisfactory solution of this problem. Even such completely normal questions of life cannot be approached with the ordinary cognitive forces, but with a thinking intensified by meditation, concentration and other soul-exercises described in my book *Knowledge of the Higher Worlds* and in my *Outline of Occult Science*, and also with transformed forces of the will.

What is attained when we try to strengthen thought by earnest meditation? I already explained to you that meditation must begin by strengthening thought to such an extent that it becomes a transformed memory. Our ordinary memory contains inner pictures which reproduce the experiences of our ordinary earthly life since our birth. Through memory, the picture of some real event stands before the soul, and that our soul-life is healthily connected with the external world in which we live, is guaranteed by the fact that we do not somehow mix up things fantastically, but that our memory-pictures indicate things which really existed.

We must therefore come to the point of being able to place before our soul, in the imaginative understanding described in the last few days, pictures which resemble our ordinary memory pictures. These pictures simply arise by our more and more bringing meditation concepts into our consciousness, and thus strengthening the soul-faculty of thinking, just as a muscle is made strong through exercise. We must reach the point of strengthening thinking to such an extent that it can live within its own content, in the same way in which we ordinarily live within our sense-experiences through our senses.

When such exercises have been made for a sufficiently long time, when we really attain to such a living way of thinking, then something develops which may be designated as a plastic form-giving, morphological way of thinking. Our thinking then contains a living essence, it has a living content which can ordinarily only be found in sense-perception. In that case we begin to notice something new: What modern natural science brings to the fore, is a source of regret to many, it constitutes materialism. But Anthroposophy which aims through its methods at penetrating into the supersensible worlds, must in a certain sphere become thoroughly "materialistic," stimulated in the right way by modern science.

This is the case if we learn to strengthen our thinking in the right way, if we can have before us, in imaginative thought, images which are just as alive as sense-perceptions and with which we deal just as freely as with sensory perceptions. When we perceive something through our senses we know unmistakably that we see Red or hear the note C sharp and that these are impressions which come to us from the external world, not impressions which rise out of our own soul. In the same way we know through imaginative thinking that the images which rise up before us are not empty phantasms produced by the soul, but that they are a living essence within, resembling sensory perception.

When we inwardly experience this emancipation from the body, this freedom which also exists in sense-perception, we also know what constitutes memory in ordinary life. When we remember something, we always plunge into our physical body; every memory-thought is connected with a parallel physical or at least etheric bodily process. We learn to know the material importance of that life which constitutes the ordinary life of memory. We then no longer ascribe the contents of memory to the independent soul, as does Bergson, the French thinker, but we know that in the ordinary memory-process the soul simply dives down into the body and that the body is the instrument which conjures up our memories. Now we know that only by *imagination* we reach the stage of being able to think independently of the body, of being able to think in ordinary life only with the soul, which we never do otherwise. In ordinary life we perceive through our senses, we abstract our thoughts from the sensory perception and retain them in our memory. But this process of retaining the thoughts in memory implies that we dive down into our body.

Imaginative knowledge alone shows us the true process of memory and that of sensory perception. Imaginative knowledge shows us what it means to live in free thoughts, emancipated from the body. It also shows us what it means to dive down into the physical organism with our thoughts, when we remember something. Even as we learn to know these things through an intensification of thinking, through an enhancement and strengthening of thought by meditation, so we may learn to know through the *will* how to pass through a kind of self-training which leads to similar results.

In ordinary life, the will only acquires a certain value when it passes over to external action; otherwise it remains mere desire, even though we may cherish the highest ideals, the most beautiful ideals, even though we may be true idealists. The highest ideals will remain mere desires, if we are not able to take hold of the external physical reality.

What characterises a *desire*, a *wish*? It has the peculiar quality of being abstracted and withdrawn from the world of reality. Symbolically one might say: When we only have desires, this is like drawing back the feelers of the soul. We then live completely within our own being, within the soul-element. But we also know that desires are, to begin with, tinged by the human temperaments. A melancholic person will have desires which differ from those of a sanguine person. The physical foundation of desires could soon be discovered by those who investigate these matters conscientiously with the aid of natural-scientific methods. The etheric foundation of desires can therefore be seen in the temperament, but their physical conditions can be perceived in the special composition of the blood or in other qualities of the bodily constitution.

This calls for that critical attitude mentioned at the beginning of my lecture; such a critical attitude shatters, I might say, many a pleasant dream. Allow me to give you a few indications which show how such pleasant dreams can be dispelled.

I certainly do not mean to be irreverent, nor do I destroy any ideal through lack of reverence, for I have a deep feeling for all the beauty contained, for instance, in the mysticism of a St. Theresa or of a St. John of the Cross. Do not think that I am second to anyone in admiring all the beauty contained in such mystical expressions. But those who have some experience of the special way in which, for instance, St. Theresa or St. John of the Cross produced their visions, know to what extent human desires have a share in these visions. They know that desires which live in the soul's depths have a share particularly in mystical experiences, and these desires may lead a spiritual investigator to study the bodily constitution of these mystics. Nothing is desecrated when a spiritual investigator draws attention to such things, when he indicates that in certain organs he discovers an inner state of excitement, that the nerves exercise a different influence on certain organs, thus producing a certain effect in the soul, which may even take on the beautiful aspect of the visions described by St. John of the Cross or by St. Theresa, or by other mystics of that type. We are far more on the right track if we seek the foundation of such visions, which are so beautiful and poetic in the case of St. Theresa and of St. John of the Cross, in certain bodily conditions than in the beholding of some nebulous mystery.

As I have said I do not wish to pull to pieces something which I revere as much as any other person in this room, but the truth must be shown, and also the critical attitude derived from an anthroposophical foundation. It must be shown that an anthroposophist above all should not fall a prey to illusions. Above all, he should be free from illusion in regard to human desires which are rooted in the human organism, desires rooted in the physical human organism which flare up, come, so to speak, to boiling point, if I may use this expression, and lead to the most beautiful visions.

A person who wishes to become a spiritual investigator in the anthroposophical sense, should not only strengthen his thinking through meditation, but he should also transform his desires through self-training.

This can be done by taking in hand systematically that which otherwise takes place as if of its own accord. Let us honestly admit that during our ordinary life we allow events to guide us far more than we ourselves guide the course of our life. In ordinary life this or that thing may influence us, and if we look back ten years into our past earthly existence, we find that the external conditions and the people whom we met, unfolded within us a side of our character which now presents a different aspect from what it was like ten years ago.

A person who earnestly strives to become an anthroposophical spiritual investigator must, in this connection, also make exercises which influence the will. The ordinary will in life acquires a meaning when directed towards external actions. But an anthroposophical spiritual investigator must apply the impulses of the will to his own development, to his own life. He should be able to pursue the following aim : " In regard to this or that characteristic or expression of life, you must change, you must become different from what you were." Though it may seem paradoxical, it is a great help if we begin to change something within us through our own initiative, through our own impulse ; if we change some strongly rooted habit, or even a small trifle. I repeat that it can be something quite insignificant, for instance, one's handwriting. If someone really strives with an iron will to change his handwriting, the application of energy required for the transformation of a habit may be compared with the strengthening of a muscle because the will is strengthened. By growing stronger and by being applied inwardly instead of outwardly, the will begins to exercise certain influences in man. The transformations in the external world once produced by the effects of the will, now become transformations within human nature.

If we do exercises of the will, as described in detail in anthroposophical books, we reach the point of transforming our life of desire, so that this becomes emancipated from the human organisation, even as our thinking emancipates itself from the body through meditation.

During the moments in which we live in anthroposophical research, we are no longer in a condition which may be described by saying that the wish is father to the thought. When we exercise this self-training, this application of education of oneself at a maturer age, our wishes and desires become an inner power which unites with the emanicipated thinking. This leads us to a real perception of the true nature of the will-impulses in ordinary life, and to a perception of the true nature of thoughts in ordinary life. Even as we ordinarily perceive red or blue, or hear C sharp or C, so we now perceive thoughts as realities; we learn to know the will-impulses objectively, that is to say, separated from our own being.

In this way we reach the point of having a right judgment of the alternating conditions of waking and sleeping. Only by rendering thought objective through exercise, as objective as a sense-perception, so that we are no longer connected with our body as in the case of a remembered thought, only with this thinking developed in free meditation, can the act of falling asleep be rightly grasped and perceived.

A person who seeks to gain insight into the normal act of falling asleep, with the aid of the ordinary cognitive forces, may set up one hypothesis after the other, but he will not be able to recognise the true nature of sleep.

This strengthened thinking which we acquire, and on the other hand our transformed desires, are those which show us that when we fall asleep we can, in a certain way, still follow the moment in which sleep takes hold of us; we look, as it were, upon the act of falling asleep and we learn to know that when we go to sleep we do not simply have before us a changed bodily condition, but that we really slip out of our body with our independent soul-life; we go out of our body and we leave something behind—namely, our thoughts.

We can leave our thoughts behind consciously, when we fall asleep, only because our thinking has been intensified. The thoughts remain behind with the body and fill it in the shape of formative forces. We notice that we have abandoned our body only with our feeling and with our will. But by perceiving with what part of the soul we leave the body, we obtain at the same time an objective certainty that we have an independent soul-essence and that we go out of the body with this independent soul-essence.

And now we know that what we leave behind on the bed on falling asleep, is not only something which can be investigated by physiology, anatomy and biology, but that it is permeated by the web of thoughts, This web of our thoughts must first be made strong enough, so that we can abandon it consciously, in the same way as we consciously turn our face away from colours and leave off looking at them. Through this strengthened thought we know that we leave behind on the bed our physical body and a body of forces containing thoughts which act like forces; we leave these bodies behind so that they may exist independently between falling asleep and waking up.

These thoughts, these morphological thoughts described to you in recent lectures, exist in our ordinary consciousness only as reflected images. They too have a reality, and with this reality they fill out our physical body as a special etheric body.

Now we know that when we fall asleep we abandon our sensory body and our thought body. (I might also say, the physical body and the etheric body, or the physical body and the body of formative forces). We abandon these bodies with our will and with our feeling. In ordinary life our constitution does not enable our consciousness to remain clear, it is not strong enough to maintain consciousness unless it is filled out by thoughts. Consciousness, such as we have it in ordinary life and in ordinary science, must unite with the body and experience within the body the thoughts of the body; only then it is fully conscious. But when the soul goes out of the body as mere feeling and will, we ordinarily become unconscious.

But a person who attains to the imaginative thinking referred to here recently, experiences the moment of falling asleep consciously, and he can produce conditions which resemble ordinary sleep, except that they are not unconscious, but that forces are at work within him and that he can really experience the organism of feeling and of the will; that is to say, he really experiences that part of his being which can emancipate itself from the body.

If we thus learn to know the moment of falling asleep, we also learn to know the moment of waking up. We now learn to judge that the moment of waking up really consists of two parts: Our attitude on waking up is the same as when a sense-impression is produced. Whenever we wake up, something must stimulate the soul. This need only be our own body, which has slept long enough and which produces this stimulus in its changed condition. But even as there is a stimulus in every sensory impression, so there is always a stimulus when we wake up, and this stimulus works upon our feeling, which left the body when we fell asleep. Even as the eyes and the ears perceive colours and sounds, so the emancipated soul now perceives through feeling something which is outside; the moment of waking up is a perception through feeling; we take hold of the body when we wake up. The independent will takes hold of the physical organism in the same way in which we ordinarily move an arm or a leg. Waking up really consists of these two acts.

In regard to falling asleep and waking up, we have now learned to know the alternating connection between the independent soul which leaves the body every night with its feeling and with its will, and the conditions in which the soul lives from the moment of waking up to the moment of falling asleep, when it is united with the body. Anthroposophical investigation is therefore based upon a strengthening of the capacities of thinking and of the will, so that we are able to observe and really perceive things which we ordinarily cannot perceive. And if in this way we are able to perceive the alternating conditions of sleeping and waking, we are then capable of passing on to something else.

For if we continue more and more in the exercises described in the recent lectures and indicated in detail in the books already mentioned we come to the point that we do not always fall asleep when we leave the body, but that we can at will draw out of the body our feeling and our will and really look back upon the body. Then the human body is as objective as a desk or a table in ordinary life. We learn to know a thing only because we are no longer connected with it, no longer penetrated by it subjectively, because it stands before us as an object.

The object which stands before us when we go out of the body with the will and with the feeling is above all the physical body. To-morrow we shall see that this perception outside the body gives us a new aspect of man's physical being. We perceive, above all, the body of formative forces, consisting of a web of thoughts, but active thoughts. We look back upon it as if it were a mirror. And then we are confronted by the strange fact that whereas formerly we were subjectively or personally connected with our thoughts, we now face this world of thoughts as if it were a photographic plate; in looking back upon our body our thoughts stand before us like a photographic plate. This is' the same as the miniature reflection of the world which we ordinarily have in our eye. Even as the eye is an organ of sight through the fact that it can reproduce the world within itself, so the etheric and the physical body which remained behind, become a reflecting apparatus, where something becomes reflected through the soul and spirit, whereas the eye only gives us a physical reflection of something outside. By leaving our thoughts behind in the physical body, we see through this mirror not only the web of thoughts, but also the world.

The course of soul-spiritual events can therefore be described in detail, when the cognitive forces are intensified through meditation and a self-training of the will, in order to gain knowledge of the supersensible worlds. Such a training enables us to develop certain conditions in which we are outside our body, but which do not resemble sleep; they constitute something which is indicated in my books as the continuity of consciousness. In higher knowledge we really go out of the body with our emancipated soul-being. We can recognise that we have left the body through the fact that the mirror of thoughts is now no longer within us, but outside. We go out of the body, yet we remain completely self-conscious, as already explained.

We are able to return into the body whenever we like; we do not fall a prey to hallucinations or visions, but we can follow the whole process with mathematical precision. Since the whole process can be observed in this way, we are also able to judge the ordinary events of earthly life when we return into the body. Now we know what it is like to dive down into the body with the emancipated soul. We not only learn to know the act of falling asleep, when we abandon the body, but now we also learn to return at will into our body with the emancipated soul.

It leaves a special impression upon us when we once experience this emancipated soul and then dive down again into the body, so that the soul becomes imprisoned by the body. The soul-spiritual world which was round about us when we were outside the body, now ceases to exist for us. We feel as if this world had vanished and that the body absorbs us as we dive into it. We also learn to know what it is like to abandon the body; we see how the thoughts go away from us, for they remain with the body, and how we abandon the body with the feeling and willing part of our soul. But in abandoning our body we feel at the same time that the spiritual world begins to rise up before us.

What knowledge have we now gained? Through the processes of waking up and of falling asleep, we have learned to know birth and death. We have experienced how the human being unconsciously abandons his physical and etheric organism with his feeling and with his will and how he returns into the body when he wakes up in the morning.

When we have made the above-mentioned exercises, we grow conscious where formerly we were unconscious, upon leaving our body. In full consciousness we now experience in advance a process which takes place when we die. And when we dive down into our physical body on returning from the spiritual world, when the thoughts outside vanish and once more appear as mere images, asserting themselves within the personality as something which is not real, then we learn to know the process of birth.

Whereas the ordinary scientific methods content themselves with the ordinary understanding, with ordinary thoughts which are applied to external observations and experiments that remain connected with us, anthroposophical investigation transforms the personality by rendering thought objective and by using the body as an all-embracing sense-organ. I might say that the body becomes one large eye. This eye, however, is outside and it is simultaneously a photographic plate.

The world into which we penetrate through spiritual investigation, the soul-spiritual world, now reflects itself in the external world as thought. An insight into completely normal processes, such as sleeping and waking, or birth and death, now enables us also to attain an inner vision of the soul-world, we perceive everything that pertains to the soul. Now our own experience enables us to distinguish whether what Professor Schleich designates as death through auto-suggestion was merely an unconscious representation, or whether what was described by Sir Oliver Lodge, was " second sight."

We can now recognise the attitude of a person who is not a conscious spiritual investigator, but whose independent soul is thrust out of the body by some abnormal conditions. This may be due to some illness of the physical body. Let us suppose that there is a lesion in an organ ; this may be quite sufficient to cause the soul-spiritual being of a person not yet capable of independent spiritual vision to be driven out of the physical body not because he falls asleep, but owing to a pathological condition of the body, so that he now obtains an imperfect perception of things which a spiritual investigator perceives consciously and methodically.

We need not deny the truth of the abnormal observations which are interesting those people to-day who wish to go beyond the sphere of ordinary, trivial facts. But we can look upon such abnormal observations critically, and such a critical attitude is due to the fact that the spiritual science of Anthroposophy is not the caricature which many people suppose it to be, but by awakening special spiritual forces and by fully recognising the scientific conscientious method acquired by humanity in the course of the past centuries, it endeavours to rise up to the supersensible worlds. And since the human being is connected with the supersensible worlds with the innermost, immortal kernel of his being, spiritual investigation alone can recognise man's mortal and immortal essence. This will be explained more fully in to-morrow's lecture.

Through the fact that the human being dives down into his eternal part, that he does not only build up an anthropology transmitting a knowledge which can only be gained through the physical body, but through the fact that he builds up an Anthroposophy, transmitting a a knowledge which man as independent being, obtains through his soul and spirit, through this fact the human being really learns to know the world in its true aspect.

The task of my next two lectures will be to describe the true being of man, his immortal, everlasting being, and the true aspect of the universe, from the stand-point indicated to-day.

MAN IN THE LIGHT OF SPIRITUAL SCIENCE

Had I not spoken to you yesterday, I could not give you to-day's lecture in the form in which I intend to give it. This is not only because this lecture is to be a continuation of yesterday's lecture, but because the facts concerning man's true being which are accessible to anthroposophical research at first appear so paradoxical that it is necessary to know the sure foundation upon which such truths are based. I think that I explained to you sufficiently clearly that both in the direction of a critical attitude and in that of a conscientious form of investigation, Anthroposophy is well able to compete with everything which modern people are accustomed to consider as a scientific method and a scientific mentality.

The subject of to-day's lecture is man's true being which, lying at the foundation of his external physical being, forms and guides it. Spiritual science above all can show that man's physical being belongs more than one generally thinks to the development of the world as such, and this connection with the whole evolution of the world will form the subject of my next lecture. Earnest-minded people, and also earnest scientists have now a different view of man's true being than a few decades ago, at the height of materialism.

But the anthroposophical facts which will now be set forth will perhaps be rejected most strongly of all by those who seek to approach the element of soul and spirit in man by adhering, as it were, to the more materialistic aspect of science.

We can see that people now begin to take an interest in the causes which produce certain abnormal soul-conditions in man which subject him to hallucinations and delusions, to suggestion and auto-suggestion. People are now specially interested in these abnormal psychic phenomena, because they can be investigated in the same way in which physical experiments are carried on, without the unfolding of the soul's dormant forces, concerning which I spoke in my last lecture. People with an abnormal spiritual life are simply approached experimentally, and the phenomena are investigated in the same way in which one makes experiments in a laboratory.

Such people, and many who are not a prey of abnormal soul-conditions, frequently believe that unusual psychic conditions, visions or hallucinations, constitute some means of penetrating more deeply into man's true being; they even think that in these abnormal conditions a kind of revelation from the real spiritual worlds can be received.

Now that man's true being can be investigated in the light of Anthroposophy, it is possible to throw light upon the real meaning of these abnormal psychic conditions. Yesterday's critical examination of certain facts may have convinced you from the very outset that anthroposophical spiritual research can confront even such abnormal phenomena with a strictly critical attitude.

Another kind of phenomenon confronts us when it is possible to perceive certain thoughts of certain people under conditions of time and of space which must undoubtedly be designated as abnormal. These cases are now being discussed quite seriously by modern scientists. Telepathy is a phenomenon of this kind. During certain psychic conditions, thoughts can be perceived through telepathy without the ordinary instrument of the senses; indeed these thoughts can even be perceived at a distance. One also speaks of telekinesis, or of certain forces proceeding from the human being which manifest themselves simply through influences at a distance, without the physical intermediary of the human being, so that it appears as if it were possible to unfold will-power and to transmit it into space without the medium of the body. In scientific circles experiments have already been made with the application of scientific methods, experiments falling under the category of teleplastic, in which phantoms and apparently physical forms appear in connection with a person, or in his close proximity. It is clearly evident that these forms consist of a fine substance, of an etheric substance, and that plastically they are permeated by something rooted as plastic force in human thinking, by something existing in human thought.

We therefore speak of telepathy, telekinesis and teleplastic. When anthroposophical spiritual science confronts these phenomena, it must again raise the critical question: Do these phenomena proceed from that part of the human being which, as explained yesterday, abandons the physical and the etheric body of man, at the moment of falling asleep, that sentient and volitional being which remains outside the body from the moment of falling asleep to the moment of waking up? Are the phenomena known as telepathy, telekinesis and teleplastic an activity of man's eternal soul-spiritual essence, of that part which we learned to know as his feeling and volitional being, or are they perhaps simply an activity of that part which remains behind on the bed during sleep, consisting solely of the physical and of the etheric body, or the body of formative forces?

If these phenomena are merely activities of the latter, they belong to that part which vanishes when we die, no matter how wonderful and extraordinary they may appear to us. For when we die, the part which remains behind on the bed during sleep, vanishes. What constitutes man's immortal, eternal being, that which abandons the physical and etheric body during sleep, as a rule also abandons the physical body when we are under some hypnotic influence, in the phenomena of telepathy, telekinesis and teleplastic. We must therefore say: These so-called wonderful phenomena cannot point to anything connected with man's eternal being; no matter how abnormal they are, they are connected with that part of his being which separates from him when he dies and which connects itself with the element of the earth. In that case they are only able to indicate a world which vanishes when the human being passes through the portal of death.

The spiritual science of Anthroposophy must therefore raise this critical objection in regard to certain phenomena which are widely recognised to-day, in the same way in which such objections had to be raised in regard to the phenomena described yesterday. It will be essential to know what Anthroposophy has to say concerning such phenomena, on the foundation of its investigations connected with man's true immortal essence.

Perhaps I may once more draw attention to the fact that through the exercises of meditation, through the exercises of thought and of the will mentioned yesterday and in other lectures which were given here, a condition can be created, particularly in regard to man's feeling and volitional part, which resembles the sleeping state, although it is radically different from sleep.

Yesterday I described to you how the sentient and volitional being in man, which is ordinarily unconscious and as it were lifeless, can be filled with inner life, with light and power, so that it is possible to create a condition in which man's feeling and volitional parts are outside the physical body as is the case during sleep, and in which these independent soul-spiritual parts can be used for anthroposophical research. In that case we no longer live in a dark world which renders us unconscious, but we are instead surrounded by a spiritual world, where the first object upon which we can look back is our physical body and our body of formative forces. This body of formative forces supplies to the inner soul-spiritual being, which has abandoned the physical and etheric body, a mirrored reflection of the world, in the form of thoughts which are now perceived as forces. Our thought-world, which was formerly connected with us, is now thrown back to us as mirrored reflections by the physical body which we left behind, so that we obtain an image of the world not because we obtain pictures of the external world through our sensory organs, for instance through the eye, which transmits us conscious experiences of the physical world, but because we now gain an image of the world's spiritual foundation through the fact that the human organism becomes as it were a sensory organ, which is now outside the human being, like any other object.

Through gradual progress in anthroposophical research, and by growing inwardly stronger and stronger, we can learn to know this being which is outside. I already explained to you that this condition in which an anthroposophical investigator lives, differs from everything which people experience in a visionary form, through hallucinations or through other psychic conditions. A spiritual investigator is always able to maintain a controlled, sound state of consciousness while investigating the higher world. He is in a condition which can really be designated as swinging to and fro from the perception of the spiritual world to that of the physical world. In other words, he can alternately live outside his physical body and his sensory perceptions, as already described, and return to his full consciousness, to his ordinary capacity of thinking, feeling and willing, so that he can judge his supersensible experiences with his everyday thinking, feeling and willing, with his normal, cool-headed common sense, with the capacities with which he ordinarily judges life in general. The results of spiritual-scientific investigations can therefore be judged quite critically; a strictly critical attitude can be adopted towards the higher experiences which confront the soul of a spiritual-scientific investigator.

In abnormal soul-conditions we do not have this alternating from one state of consciousness to another. People who have visions or hallucinations cannot return at will, when they consider it best, to their ordinary, calm state of mind, through an effort of the will; that is to say, they cannot return at will into their physical body. They are led into such abnormal conditions by an involuntary sub-conscious element which produces hallucinations and visions, and the total absence of criticism in regard to their abnormal conditions is a fact which must be indicated over and over again, whenever the results of anthroposophical, spiritual-scientific research are brought into connection with things which have a visionary or hallucinatory character.

By swinging to and fro from a higher state of consciousness to the ordinary way of seeing things and to ordinary consciousness, we more and more attain the capacity to look back upon our physical and etheric bodies, which now exist objectively outside our soul-spiritual kernel; we look back upon the physical and etheric bodies with forces developed in the sentient and volitional part of our being. By ascending to the imaginative state of consciousness, we now really learn to know what we have before us as a picture of another world. The important point to be borne in mind is that through the imaginative and inspirational knowledge described in my last lectures, we really learn to form a judgment upon the physical body and the body of formative forces, which we now see from outside.

To use a comparison, it is as if we first had before us a picture and were to learn the corresponding reality which it represents by gaining a knowledge of the laws of perspective. But the reality which we gather from an ordinary picture is, after all, only an inner soul-experience, whereas the larger perspective in which we objectively look upon the physical body and the body of formative forces, is a real experience of facts. For we learn to know that the physical body and the body of formative forces contain, in an image, what we ourselves were, before descending into the physical world through birth or conception.

In this perspective, something frees itself from what we thus see before us and leads us back into the spiritual world through which we passed before we united ourselves through birth or conception with the physical substance given to us by our parents and ancestors, and transmitted by the physical stream of heredity here on earth. We can survey the soul-spiritual world which surrounds us before we came down into an earthly existence; it is the world which contains the forces that became united with our physical form, transmitted by our parents and forefathers.

We now learn to know ourselves in our pre-existence, in our pre-natal condition, and the characteristic fact which rises up before us is that in this picture representing man's pre-existent being we actually see the world reversed, in comparison with a physical perspective. In a physical perspective we see the nearest objects most clearly of all, and the further off they lie, the more they grow indistinct; this characterises the perspective of the spatial world.

But matters appear reversed in the perspective which now rises up out of the human being that remained behind. The things most closely related with our physical life on earth are those which are most familiar to our present experience; in reality we do not know our own inner being during our physical life on earth. Our physical life on earth is something which darkens our eternal being, our innermost kernel. But when we look into the pre-existent world, the things which we perceive spiritually first of all are not those which are most familiar to us in earthly life, not the closest, nearest things, but we first perceive the more distant things. If we have ascended through the three stages which can be developed through exercises as higher stages of knowledge, in accordance with descriptions contained in my book *Knowledge of the Higher Worlds*, then Imagination, Inspiration and Intuition really enable us to obtain a complete soul-spiritual picture of the universe, leading us back to a past life on earth.

Even as a physical perspective is limited in the distance, so the image which we obtain of a world in which we lived in a pre-existent condition is limited by a past earthly life which opens out to us through intuition. The spiritual science of Anthroposophy does not speak of anything fantastic nor of some logical inference when it speaks of the repeated lives on earth, for this knowledge is gained through cognition, it is a fact which presents itself to the real spiritual vision. But this spiritual vision, this spiritual perception, must first be drawn out of the depths of the soul. We then obtain a positive knowledge of the fact that man's physical body, man's etheric body or the body of formative forces, plastically contain those essential forces which lived in the human being during the time between death and a new birth.

This also explains that we have developed out of a spiritual world into the physical world. Within the physical body, which man carries not merely as a covering but as a kind of instrument, and within the etheric body, containing the living forces which lie at the foundation of the organs, of metabolism and growth, within these bodies which appear objectively before us in spiritual vision, lives the soul's inner kernel, which is plastically moulded into them, the soul's essential being, as it has developed in a soul-spiritual world since the last death until the last birth. When we abandon the physical and etheric body with our sentient-volitional being, we learn to know what we thus leave behind us, as the last thing, as it were, to which we longingly turned on growing old, so to speak, in the spiritual world; the last thing to which we turned in our existence between death and a new birth before " dying " in the spiritual world. Even as we perceive that our physical body begins to fade at a certain age, on approaching death through old age, so we perceive that our soul-spiritual being begins to fade in the spiritual world in which we then live.

This fading away of our soul-spiritual being reveals itself in our longing for the physical world, for a corporeal physical incarnation. Consequently that part which lives in our physical and etheric body constitutes, as it were, the last phase of our existence above in the spiritual world. During our sleep, when we go out of our physical body as sentient-volitional beings, we leave behind our past.

What do we then take with us? If we realise the fact that we leave behind our past, we can also realise the fact that what is ordinarily an unconscious experience from the moment of falling asleep to the moment of waking up, is that part of man's being which passes through the portal of death and re-enters a soul-spiritual world. That part of man's being which could not dive down into the physical and etheric body, which remained behind, as it were, that part goes out every night when we fall asleep, and it also passes again as a being of feeling and will, through the portal of death. Thus eternity becomes guaranteed to man through this real perception.

And if we now look back to what is striven for without any understanding by a certain modern scientific direction which clings to external, superficial facts in order to investigate phenomena such as telepathy, teleplastic and telekinesis, we see that these phenomena are really connected with man's past, with the part which perishes when he dies, with something which cannot constitute anything pertaining to the real supersensible world, but only to forces which are connected with the human being in the physical realm of the earth.

If we vividly imagine that part of our pre-existent being which descends into a physical embodiment through conception and birth, we can understand that in its development it absorbs the forces and substances transmitted by the hereditary stream; it also takes in forces during the course of earthly existence which are absorbed through the process of nutrition and breathing and through everything which the human being receives from the external world. The human being only exists as a full reality in that being that descends into physical embodiment from a pre-existent, pre-natal life. Within the mother's body it already enters into and envelops itself with physical matter and later on draws in substance through breathing, nutrition, and so forth.

Only when the human being is awake, only during this normal condition of life, the part which man thus incorporates into himself enters into connection with his true being, with his sentient and volitional being, through the physical and etheric bodies. When the human being is awake, there exists a normal connection between his sentient-volitional being and his thinking capacity, which is bound up, as we already have seen, with the etheric body and with the physical body.

Let us now suppose that in a hypnotic condition man's sentient and volitional being is drawn out of the physical and the etheric body. The hypnotised man whom we then have before us, consists merely of the body of formative forces and of the physical body, with all the physical substances and forces which he has absorbed from the external physical world. There are many reciprocal relationships between these substances and forces and the environing world, and all this enters the human being. When the sentient, volitional part of man is outside the physical and etheric body, it is possible to observe the influence of these physical substances. Through anthroposophical investigation, we discover that this does not pertain to man's immortal essence, to man's inner kernel, but that it is something which pertains to the external world and which unites with his immortal part, something which became incorporated into it in the past.

The same thing can appear if the person succumbs to some kind of illness. In a normal condition, a diseased organ can be felt through pain, sickness, and so forth. This is the case when the volitional-sentient being is rightly connected with the physical and etheric body. But if the physical or even the etheric body is somehow deformed by illness, then through the disease of some organ, some inner member of the soul and spirit, the sentient-volitional being in man dives down more deeply into his animal-physical nature than is the case in a normal state of consciousness, when the memories are only thrown back like mirrored reflections. When the physical organs are sound, the human being dives down into his physical body only to a certain degree; but if the organs are diseased, if only *one* organ is diseased, the soul-spiritual being not only dives down as far as the point where pain arises in the normal course of an illness, but it dives down deeper still. The soul-spiritual being unites with the physical organism. Whereas in the ordinary course of life man's sentient-volitional being is normally connected only with the sensory and with the nervous system, it now becomes connected with the lower animalic organs and with the vegetative organs, so that the involuntary conditions of hallucination and of visionary experience arise. One sees that hallucinations and visionary experiences, as well as other similar conditions, are entirely united with man's physical and etheric bodies, and that therefore, they can only be experiences which vanish when the human being dies and can throw no light whatever upon the supersensible world in which we live between death and a new birth. There is, however, one phenomenon attested by sound scientific research, namely that in a mediumistic condition it is possible to perceive thoughts of a certain importance, and sometimes one can be amazed at the very clever thoughts voiced by a medium in trance, i.e. by a person who is in a kind of hypnotic state, thoughts which would not be possible to him in a normal state of consciousness.

Does this fact contradict the explanations given above? It does not contradict them, because not only the physical body, but also the etheric body can exercise an influence in space, without the medium of the physical body. Even quite normal people, particularly those who have a spark of genius in them, may produce thoughts and phantasies which are not limited to the body of formative forces, and because these transcend normal life and even the human being himself, they go out, as it were, into the universal cosmic ether, which we shall learn to know in our next lecture.

We can really say that the artistic thoughts which transcend normal life continue to swing in the universal cosmic ether, thoughts which appear —if I may use this expression—in superhuman artistic creations and experiences. These thoughts whirr about in the cosmic ether.

People who prepare themselves through exercises of the will and meditation described yesterday, know that man does not only produce things physically, by physical deeds. They know that thoughts which are not required for the maintenance of individual life (individual life requires thinking forces which change into forces of growth) are imparted to the universal cosmic ether. When the etheric body is in some pathological condition, when it is deformed or when it becomes mediumistic through trance, then the thoughts which whirr about in the cosmic ether and which do not enter our normal consciousness, can penetrate into a person deprived of his soul-spiritual part and manifesting as a medium. And when, for instance, the thoughts of a dead person imparted to the universal ether manifest themselves through a medium, it is possible to believe that one is really perceiving the thoughts, the present thoughts of the departed soul, whereas in reality one only perceives the echo of thoughts rayed out before death, when that person was still living on the earth.

This is what should always be borne in mind, through a sound, critical, spiritual-scientific attitude. We should be aware whether we merely confront thought-echoes, or whether the development of supersensible forces really enables us to penetrate into the supersensible world to which we belong after death and before birth. Telepathy is merely an etheric transmisson of thoughts with the exclusion of the senses. In telekinesis certain forces producing changes in the physical body through nutrition or through other physical substances, are stimulated to action in space without a physical intermediary. The human being only consists of about 10 per cent of solid substance; he is a liquid column in regard to the remaining 90 per cent. But he also consists of finer materials, extending to the etheric. In a pathological condition, when an organ is diseased, so that the soul-spiritual part dives down too deeply into the animalic part, it is possible to impart thoughts with the aid of these finer substances which are rayed out in a certain way. Teleplastic also arises in this way. In teleplastic the fine substantiality which is rayed out can be given form, and these forms moulded by thought may even be filled with light and radiance. Plastic forms arise, such as those described in the books of Schrenk-Notzing and of others. These works are always on a scientific level, and preclude any idea of swindle or fraud.

But in all these cases we simply have to do with activities proceeding from that part of man's being which perishes when he dies. They do not supply us with anything which can lead us into the real supersensible world.

We penetrate into the real supersensible world when we are able to observe things outside the body with the aid of our sentient-volitional being, through a systematic training and intensification of our normal soul-capacities and by maintaining our normal state of consciousness. In that case we can survey the past which appears in the physical and in the etheric body, the past which we rayed out from a spiritual world and which plastically moulded our physical and etheric substances.

And since we first perceive most clearly of all, so to speak, the things which lie further off, and only gradually the things in closer proximity, we are able to see as far as the point of our death in a preceding life. As described in my *Theosophy* this perception of our pre-existent, pre-natal life, enables us to give a description of man's experiences after death. We then describe things, as it were, from a reversed perspective. And thus all the descriptions which I have given you on man's conditions and experiences after death, are based upon that spiritual perception which can be attained in the manner I described yesterday and again to-day.

One can say that it is impossible to gain any direct experience of the higher worlds unless we first acquire it through an earnest striving after knowledge. Through the strengthening of thought, as described yesterday, we must create the possibility of being outside the body in a fully conscious state and of looking back upon it. This can only be attained by intensifying our thinking power. But we must also learn to make distinctions. Everything which comes from a preceding life lies open to our perception, but everything which pertains to the future is only accessible to inner experience.

These inner experiences are meagre in comparison with the mighty supersensible tableau of pre-existent life which confronts us, for our prenatal existence can really form the content of a fully developed science. But anything which we can gather concerning the future will very much depend upon the inner strengthening of our sentient-volitional being, when it is outside the body. This sentient-volitional being can also be observed in its course of development during the physical life on earth, as it gradually matures for a higher state of existence after death. Differences become evident, if we first observe that part of man which ordinarily abandons him unconsciously during sleep, in a more youthful stage of life and then observe it in a maturer stage. The sentient-volitional being which abandons the body of a younger person during sleep, is more filled with a reflective, thoughtful element. We observe that it unconsciously reverberates the thoughts which the human being harbours. When a person grows older, he no longer carries out of his physical body so many thoughts when crossing the portal of sleep, but he takes out with his sentient-volitional being into the external world, forces of character, forces contained in his developed impulses of the will.

We can therefore say: During our earthly life, we gradually change from a being in whom thoughts are the predominant element, into a being who manifests in his soul-spiritual part more the echo of forces which constitute his character. Essentially speaking, we do not pass through the portal of sleep with our thoughts, for we leave them behind when we fall asleep and they shine forth through the physical body. We leave behind the thoughts which animated us during our earthly life from birth to death. We learn to look upon them as external thought-forces of the world; later on, after death, we learn to know them as an external world. We pass through the portal of sleep with these forces which have formed our character, which constitute our inner moral development. If we wish to interpret rightly every phase in the perspective which appears to us in the world of our pre-existent life, we must first gain this capacity through the development of our normal soul-forces.

In the previous lecture, I have already described to you that when a person intensifies his life of thought through meditation and concentration, so that he can live in thoughts in the same way in which he ordinarily lives in sensory impressions, in an inner life of thoughts as powerful, living and intensive as the life of the soul when it surrenders to sensory impressions, then he attains to imaginative knowledge. This inner thought-life intensified to the stage of imaginative consciousness, now enables him to confront not only the memory tableau of his past earthly life up to the present moment, but he surveys everything pertaining to his physical earthly organism, shaped and moulded by the body of formative forces. His first supersensible experience is to look back from the present moment upon his whole earthly life, as far as childhood, in the form of a mighty tableau.

I already mentioned in my last lectures that the tableau which can thus be experienced, resembles in some points a fact which even serious scientists discuss to-day, for it is sufficiently attested that such a picture arises when a person is in mortal danger, with hardly any hope of escape. A drowning person, for instance, may experience in a great tableau that which constitutes the etheric time-body of formative forces; he looks upon this body.

Supersensible knowledge enables us to obtain this same survey, which constitutes the first experience after death through the right interpretation of the perspective described to you of our pre-existent, pre-natal life.

Then we recognise the fact that when the human being passes through the portal of death, he perceives for a short time, lasting only a few days (approximately as long as a person is able, in accordance with his organisation, to do without sleep for a few days) a kind of tableau, giving him a survey of his past earthly life in a kind of thought-web, but consisting of pictures. We obtain, for a short time, this survey of our earthly life, when we pass through the portal of death. I might say, that we face our earthly life without the participation of our feelings and of our will, purely in a kind of passive survey; after death, we learn to know this first condition as I have described it.

We must first gain this experience through supersensible knowledge, through meditation and concentration, etc. But we require another kind of training if we wish to interpret rightly in this tableau the connection between our past earthly life and the life after death.

In our earthly life, and even in ordinary science, we generally surrender ourselves passively to the external world with our thoughts, feelings and will-impulses. We keep pace with the external world. We experience the Yesterday, then in connection with it the To-day, and a little later, the To-morrow. And the inner reflections of our thoughts, feelings and will-impulses, developed within the soul, are connected with the external course of time, as a continued natural experience. This, as it were, gives our ordinary thinking and feeling a kind of support, but man's thinking cannot reach the required degree of intensification, enabling it to make supersensible investigations, if it passively submits to the external course of time. Other exercises are now needed; we must try—if I may use this expression—to think backwards. When the day is over, we should pass in review all that we have seen during the day, but we should not do this in the form of thoughts, nor critically, but in the form of pictures; we should, as it were, see everything once more, in the same way in which we see things through our phantasy but from evening to morning in reversed sequence. We should acquire a certain practice in this thinking backwards in the form of pictures. It is relatively easy to think backwards larger portions of the day, but in order to have a reversed picture of the day's course, atomistically small portions must also be surveyed backwards, and this must be practised for a long time.

We can then advance to other exercises; for instance, we can seek help by trying to experience a drama backwards, from the Fifth Act back to the First, try experiencing melodies inwardly, by hearing, as it were, soul-spiritually. We can thus attain the capacity of looking upon our life's memories (this is something different from the life-tableau described above) by conjuring them up before our soul backwards, in the form of imaginative pictures, so that our whole life stands before us, from the present moment back into the past. By making such exercises, we emancipate our thinking from the external course of time. The deeply rooted habit of following the course of time with our thinking and feeling must be overcome. By forcefully thinking backwards we are gradually enabled to make use of a far greater and stronger capacity of thinking than that employed for a merely passive thinking. Our thinking power can be essentially strengthened just by this way of thinking backwards.

And we then discover something which undoubtedly seems paradoxical to the normal consciousness and to the ordinary understanding. But in the same way in which one looks upon the physical world with conceptions flowing in the stream of time, so one gradually comes to look upon the spiritual world, when one's thinking has been emancipated from its connection with the external course of time.

This produces a further capacity which enables one to observe the new experiences and to interpret rightly, from the perspective already described, the things connected with the life-tableau which one sees for a few days after death.

After this life-tableau, we can see how man once more passes through his life, by living through it backwards in very real and vivid pictures. Man experiences, as it were, the soul-world before experiencing the spirit world. He lives backwards through life, from his death to his birth, but more quickly than during his earthly existence from birth to death. He lives through this life backwards.

The capacity to perceive this is acquired by the already mentioned exercises of thinking backwards. And now we gain a conception of how after death man experiences in this reversed course of soul-life everything that he experienced here on earth in his physical body. But he now experiences all these things with his *soul*, and he can see everything that harmed his progress morally. By this very living backwards through time, he can now survey from a higher standpoint what he would like to change in life. For he can see how certain moral defects handicapped his development towards perfection. But since he now experiences all this in a living way, it does not remain in the realm of thought. In this reversed course of soul-life—I might say, in this soul-life which he develops backwards, thought does not remain abstract, for abstract thoughts were left behind with death; thought now develops as a thinking *force*. It becomes an impulse which leads the human being to make amends during his next earthly life, in some way to experience facts which are opposite to those which now come before his soul. In the soul there develops something which in the next life appears in the form of subconscious longings to approach this or that experience in life. In this living backwards through our past life, we develop the desire to experience in our next earthly life events or facts which counterbalance those which we have gone through in the past. And so this reversed course of development contains the seed of something which we unconsciously bring with us when we are born again, something which can be described somewhat in the following way.

This is generally not accessible to the ordinary consciousness; nevertheless it lives in man. But observe merely with your plain common sense something which supersensible research establishes as a fact—namely, *how* we approach some decisive fact in life.

Let us suppose that during one of our earthly lives we meet another human being in our 30th or 35th year (I will take a decisive event) and that he becomes our life-companion with whom we wish to share our further destiny in life, that we discover that our souls harmonise. An ordinary materialistic person will say that this was pure chance. Deeper minds—there are many, and they can be traced in history—have however reflected a little over this problem : If we now look back in life from this decisive event, if we survey what preceded it, what came before that, and still further back ... we find that the course of our life tending towards this event followed a definite plan. Sometimes we discover that an event which we thus experience in our life, a fact having such an incisive influence upon our life, appears like the organic conclusion of a well defined plan.

If we have first constructed such a plan hypothetically and lead it back as far as our birth, and if we then survey it with the aid of cognitive forces developed through meditation, retrospective thinking, will-exercises, we must really say to ourselves : This hypothetical plan which you constructed, may sometimes appear like a mere phantasy, but it is not always so. Precisely for decisive facts in life, it often reveals itself as of greatest importance that the human being carries within him from his birth a subconscious longing, and that guided by this longing, which he perhaps interprets quite differently in the various epochs of his life, he makes the first step, the second step and all the steps which finally lead him to the event which he formed as a seed during his retrospective experience after death and which carries him through his new earthly life as an undefined longing. We thus shape our destiny ourselves in an unconscious way. This enables us to recognise what we encounter during our earthly existence, this destiny or Karma, as it was designated in the ancient, instinctive, clairvoyant wisdom of the Orient. This destiny, on which our happiness and unhappiness, our joy and pain in life depends, we can learn to recognise by looking upon the sequence of our earthly lives.

A man will naturally very soon be inclined to say : How do matters then stand in regard to *freedom* ?—For if man is guided by destiny, how do matters stand in regard to human freedom ?— Indeed, a solution of the question of destiny can only be gained by striving earnestly with the problem of freedom. At this point allow me to insert something personal, for it undoubtedly has an objective significance. In the early nineties of the past century I wrote my *Philosophy of Spiritual Activity*. The task of this book was to establish the experience, the fact of freedom. From man's own inner experiences I sought to characterise the consciousness of freedom as an absolute certainty. And the subsequent explanations which I have tried to give as a partial solution of the problem of destiny, such as the sketch which I gave you now, I consider to be in entire harmony with the descriptions of human freedom. Those who study my book *Philosophy of Spiritual Activity* will find however I was obliged to renounce speaking of freedom of the human will at first, and to speak instead of a freedom experienced in thought, in pure thinking emancipated from the senses. In thoughts which consciously arise in the human soul as an ethical, moral ideal, in thoughts which have the strength to influence the human will and to lead it to action, in such thoughts there is freedom. We can speak of human freedom when we speak of human actions shaped by man's own free thinking, when he reaches the point, through a moral self-training, of not allowing his actions to be influenced by instincts, passions, emotions or by his temperament, but only by the devoted love for an action. In this devoted love for an action, can develop something which proceeds from the ideal strength of pure ethical thinking. This is a really free action.

Spiritual science now enables us to discover that during sleep thinking as such, the thinking which lies at the foundation of free ethical actions, remains behind in the mirroring physical body. It is thus something that man experiences between birth and death. Even if human life were not of immense value also from other aspects, the inclusion of the impulse of freedom in our experiences between birth and death renders our life on earth valuable in itself. In our physical existence on earth we attain freedom by developing thought as such, when thought loses the plastic force which it still has within the etheric body and is developed as pure thinking in the consciousness which we have in ordinary life.

In the early nineties of the past century I was therefore obliged to set forth a very daring thought in my *Philosophy of Spiritual Activity*. I had to speak of moral impulses in the form of ethical ideas and had to explain that these do not come to us from Nature, but through intuition. At that time I spoke of " moral phantasy." Why ? —In my *Philosophy of Spiritual Activity* I explained that these ethical motives stream into man from the spiritual world, but at first in the form of pictures. He receives them from the spiritual world as intuition.

But we thus come, as it were, to the other pole of what we experience here, in the physical world. Everywhere in the realm of Nature we discover necessity, if we look out into it with our sound common sense and with a scientific mentality. If we look into the world of moral impulses, then we discover freedom, but to begin with, freedom in the form of mere thought, of pure thinking, in the intuition that lives in the thinking activity. At first we do not know how these moral forces enter the will, for we perceive ethical intuitions unconsciously. So we have on the one hand Nature, to which we belong through our actions, and on the other hand our ethical experience. Through natural science alone, we should lose the possibility to ascribe reality and world-creative forces to these ethical intuitions. We experience Nature as it were, in its whole dense grossness, in its necessity. And then we experience freedom, but we experience it in the finely-woven impulses of thinking which reach the imaginative stage, and since these do not form part of Nature and can be experienced in free activity, we know that they come from the spiritual world, as I have indicated in my *Philosophy of Spiritual Activity*.

But something must now be inserted between these intuitions which are entirely of a picture-nature and unreal and which only acquire reality through ethical life, between these intuitions and the objective cognition of Nature and its laws. It is imagination and inspiration, which arise in the way I have described, that now insert themselves. In that case intuition too undergoes a change. The impulse which first appeared only in pure thinking, becomes as it were condensed into a spiritual reality.

In this newly acquired intuition, gained through imagination and inspiration, we do not learn to know our present Ego, but the Ego that passes through repeated lives on earth and that carries our destiny through these repeated earthly lives. In passing through these repeated earthly lives which moulded our destiny, we are not free. Yet we can always insert free actions into this web of destiny during our different lives on earth. Just because the imaginative intuition enables us to experience ethical impulses (not as realities, but as something which we can freely accept), we can weave freedom into the web of destiny during a definite earthly life. The fact that destiny bears us from one earthly life into another, does not render us less free than the fact that a steamer can carry us from Europe to America. Our future is determined by the decision to travel arrived at in Europe; yet within certain limits we are always free, and we can move about freely while we are in America. This is how destiny is borne from one earthly life into another. But to the world of facts which we thus experience during our repeated lives on earth, we can insert what wells up out of freedom during a definite life.

And so we see that those who struggle with the problem of freedom and see the solution in the contemplation of ethical ideas which can at first only be grasped through moral phantasy, but which penetrate from the spiritual world into the physical world of man,—we see that those who in this way acquire an understanding for the problem of freedom, have prepared themselves thereby for the comprehension of destiny, which enters human life almost like a necessity.

If we attain this intuition and understand the interweaving of destiny and freedom and thus intensify still further the forces acquired through meditation, concentration, retrospective thought, etc., we are able to contemplate, that is to interpret further the facts which appear to us in the spiritual perspective.

What now is attached to this retrospective experience is a life which takes its course in a purely spiritual sphere in which we now live towards a subsequent life on earth. In this spiritual sphere our experience is just the reverse of our experience during our earthly life. Here on earth, our inner experiences can, to begin with, only be perceived inwardly, as pictures. We do not experience our inner being with our ordinary consciousness, for our waking consciousness makes us experience the external world. We look out, as it were, from our own centre into the environing spatial world, into the spatial sphere, the external world. We are within ourselves and the external world is outside.

During our existence between death and a new birth this conception is just reversed: We are now centred in a world which constituted our external world here on earth, and the external world on earth now becomes a kind of inner world.

The inner world of human nature, which was not accessible to us during our earthly life, can now be experienced as an external world. And during our life between death and a new birth, our inner being becomes the world! And the world becomes our Ego.

And inasmuch as we experience something which is now higher than the world which surrounds us here on earth (for man is the crown of creation, he bears within himself a sphere which is higher than the surrounding world), we have within us a more valuable world during our existence between death and a new birth. The world which we thus experience as our own environment, but which is actually the mysterious world of man's inner being, is experienced creatively. In the spiritual world we experience these forces creatively, in common with higher spiritual Beings that surround our soul-spiritual being, in the same way in which the kingdoms of Nature, the plants, the animals and the minerals, surround our physical being on earth.

In communion with these spiritual Beings, we experience the forces out of which we gradually mould not only our destiny, the seed of our destiny, but also our prototype in the soul-spiritual world. This is the real prototype, that soul-spiritual being, which after a certain time is filled with the longing to incorporate again, to send down the prototype into a physical body, the prototype which it first shaped in living thoughts in the spiritual world. And since it must become united with a physical body, since it can only reach perfection in a physical body, this soul-spiritual being is filled with the impulse and longing to reincarnate here on earth. Out of the spirit comes that being from an existence lying before birth, or before conception, and unites with the physical body.

A true conception of the way in which man develops here on earth as a physical being (more exact details will be given the day after tomorrow) can only be gained if we can grasp the fact that what develops in the mother's body is only something which receives from a higher world the real being of man.

Natural science has a certain ambition and dream, consisting in the hope to discover one day the complicated chemical structure of cells, indeed of the most perfect cells, the reproductive cells, the germ cells of the human embryo. The spiritual science of Anthroposophy approaches this same problem, but with quite different means and from entirely different points of view. And Anthroposophy is able, in a certain way, to point out the direction in which to seek that which develops in the mother's body as germinative cell of the human embryo. Here we do not come across complicated chemical combinations, but in reality with a chaotic state of matter. We do not have before us a highly complicated chemical combination or some molecular structure, but a chaotic condition, a chaotic vortex of the ordered structure which exists in a crystal and in a chemical molecule. In the germinative cell matter is not developed to a further organisation, but it is pushed down into chaos, and from the corresponding substance, from the substance which becomes chaotic, then develops something which can now receive what comes down to it from above; the supersensible man coming from the spiritual worlds.

The development of physical man will only be grasped if physical research is brought to the point of being able to see how the physical human germ by leading matter back to chaos, becomes capable of receiving the soul-spiritual germ which comes down from pre-existence. Only in this way it is possible to understand how the soul-spiritual part descending from the soul-spiritual world becomes united through conception and up to birth with what has de-materialised itself in the germ, in the early embryonic stage. All who carefully study the form and development of the embryo can find, even in its physical development, the confirmation of to-day's description, whereas this embryonic development will always remain a riddle to those who cannot consider it in this way.

To be sure, if we really wish to know man's true being we must receive from supersensible research what also belongs to man. On earlier occasions, I have, for instance, pointed out that in the science dealing with the lower kingdoms, people would everywhere consider foolish things which are looked upon as wisdom in the investigation of the human being.

I already gave you the example of a magnet-needle, with one of its ends pointing North and the other one South. Now it would certainly not enter anyone's mind to say that the forces which it manifests are only contained in the magnet needle, in the space occupied by that needle. One looks upon the earth itself as a great magnet which exercises its influence upon the magnet-needle and which determines its direction. The magnet-needle is included in the structure of the whole earth-organism.

In this case one transcends the single thing, in order to recognise the great comprehensive whole and its inter-relation with the single object. Yet in the case of man one seeks to recognise everything pertaining to man by studying the development of the germ cell through the microscope and by contemplating only what is enclosed within the human skin ! Just as little as the forces of the magnet can be explained through the magnet, just as little is it possible to know what develops in the human being if one does not bring him in relation with the whole world, not only with the spatial world, but also with the world of time ; it is not possible to understand the human being unless one goes back to his pre-existent, pre-natal being, revealing itself, as described, to supersensible vision. We learn to know this pre-existent being when man lays aside his physical body here on earth, when we see his etheric body dissolving in the cosmic ether—we see this pre-existent being passing once more through the portal of death in order to begin a new cycle leading to a further adjustment of life's facts and to a higher perfection.

This is how man stands within the evolution of the world, if we look upon his essence as such. What we now receive, inasmuch as we bear our soul-spiritual being down to earth, pertains to the evolution of the world and must be included in the cosmic development, as we shall see in the next lecture. The human being will only be understood if what has been explained to-day is at the same time inserted into the being and becoming, that is, into the whole cosmic development. For man can only recognise the world by recognising *himself*. And what constitutes the universe is reflected in earthly life, and the human being lives through it after death and before birth. From this sphere he takes the forces which he himself incorporates with his physical body at birth or conception. The universe and man belong together not only outwardly, but also inwardly. Man bears the world within himself; the world as a totality forms man's being. The question which we have raised is therefore partially answered to-day; it will be fully answered, to the extent allowed to-day by science, in my next lecture.

In conclusion let me say a few more words. I want it to be really understood that the facts explained by the spiritual-scientific investigator are based upon the development of forces which ordinarily remain unconscious to the soul, but that from the anthroposophical standpoint, the spiritual-scientific investigator proceeds in such a way that he clothes the facts obtained through supersensible vision in the thoughts which are ordinarily used in science. Everywhere he takes his thoughts with him. For his research-work must always be accompanied by that pendulum swinging from the supersensible to the physical world. He must always stand as his own critic by the side of his higher being endowed with super-sensible vision. Consequently even those who have not made such exercises can really examine and test with their own thinking all the facts brought forward by the spiritual investigator; they can test them with their own thinking, if only they follow in an unprejudiced way their own sound common sense. It is really not true that only a spiritual investigator could test the facts brought forward by spiritual research. In the present time, we have grown too accustomed to the manner of thinking connected with external matter, with the external sequence of natural facts, and we find that a spiritual investigator cannot supply proofs valid for this way of thinking. But those who penetrate into all the circumstances, understand the connection existing between the ordinary sound common sense and the methodically developed understanding of science, of external science. And those who think critically, and with sufficient lack of prejudice test all the facts advanced by the spiritual investigator, will be able to do this, even though they themselves are not endowed with supersensible vision. The spiritual investigator brings forward everything in such a way that it can be tested. Those who say that a spiritual investigator merely relates what he sees through his own supersensible vision without supplying any proofs, resembles a person who is accustomed to think that everything which he finds on earth stands upon a firm ground, and when someone explains to him a solar system immediately asks: What then does that rest upon?

Perhaps he does not perceive that it rests upon itself, that it is freely borne by its own forces. A person who asks for proofs resembles one who asks: On what foundation does a solar system stand then? He resembles such a person if he asks for ordinary proofs and means such proofs as can only be asked for the external sensory world, where it is possible to discover, without any proof, the things which the senses perceive, the existence of which can be proved through the senses.

But human thinking does not only exist for this purpose; human thinking can also rise to things which are demonstrable not only through sound common sense upon the foundation of sensory experience, but to things which are carried by their own inner forces, like a spiritual planetary system. Try to examine in this way, by applying it to anthroposophical spiritual investigation, the results obtained by such a self-supporting, self-demonstrating thinking; you will then find that the facts advanced by a spiritual investigator are inwardly just as surely founded—even without the so-called external supports—as a planetary system supports itself freely in cosmic space, and that a supporting foundation is only needed by what is terrestrial and heavy. This however must be remembered: that thinking must also become really free, it must become something which can carry itself inwardly, if sound human intelligence is to find a proof for the facts which spiritual research advances in connection with the being of man and the evolution of the world. That from this standpoint it is possible to prove everything, I shall hope to develop in my next lecture on the nature of world evolution, following the explanations now given on the nature of man.

WORLD-DEVELOPMENT IN THE LIGHT OF SPIRITUAL SCIENCE

The thoughts which I have been putting before you, will show you that the acquisition of real supersensible knowledge entails above all, with the aid of the exercises already described, that the two sides of human nature which are usually inexactly designated as man's inner and outer being should be distinctly separated. Perhaps it may be pointed out that in ordinary consciousness one does not make an exact distinction between man's inner and outer being, when speaking of these. The way in which I characterised the going out of man's sentient and volitional being during sleep and the becoming conscious in supersensible knowledge outside the physical body, shows us that just this supersensible knowledge enables us to separate distinctly those parts which are usually described vaguely in ordinary consciousness as man's outer and inner being.

I might say that by this separation man's inner world becomes his outer world, and what we usually consider as his outer world becomes his inner world.

What takes place in that case? During sleep, man's sentient and volitional being abandons what we have called his physical body and etheric body, or the body of formative forces, and then this sentient-volitional being looks back upon the physical body and the etheric body as if they were objects. We showed that in this retrospection the whole web of thought appears outside man's inner being. The world of thought which fills our ordinary consciousness and which reflects the external world, does not go out with man's true inner being in falling asleep, but remains behind with the physical body, as the true forces of the etheric body. In this way we were able to grasp that during our waking state of consciousness we cannot grow conscious of that part which goes out during sleep and which remains unconscious for the ordinary consciousness. (Self-observation can easily convince us that during our ordinary waking consciousness the world of thoughts produces this waking state of consciousness).

In that part of the human being which goes out of the physical and the etheric bodies during sleep, there is a dull twilight-life, and we only learn to know this inner being of man when supersensible knowledge fills it, as it were, with light and with warmth, when we are just as conscious within this inner being as we are ordinarily conscious within our physical body. But we also learn to know why we have an unconscious life during our ordinary sleeping condition. Consciousness arises when we dive down into our physical and etheric bodies at the moment of waking up. And by diving down into the physical body, we make use of the senses which connect us with the external world. As a result, the sensory world awakes and we thus grow conscious in it.

In the same way we dive down into our etheric or life-body, that is to say, into our world of thoughts, and we grow conscious within our thoughts. Ordinary consciousness is therefore based upon the fact that we use the instruments of our physical body, and that we make use, so to speak, of the etheric body's web of formative forces. In ordinary life, man's true inner being, woven out of feeling and will, is not in a position to attain consciousness, because it has no organs. By making the thought- and will-exercises of which I have spoken, we endow the soul itself with organs. This soul-element, which is at first indistinct in our ordinary consciousness, acquires plastic form, even as our physical body and our etheric body acquire plastic form in the senses and in the organs of thought. Man's real soul-spiritual being therefore obtains a plastic form.

In the same measure in which it is moulded plastically and acquires (if I may use this paradoxical expression) soul-spiritual sense-organs, the world of soul and spirit rises up round our inner being. That part of our being which ordinarily lives in a dull twilight existence and which can only perceive an environing world, namely the physical world, when it uses the physical and etheric organs of perception, thus acquires plastic form and enters into connection with a world which always surrounds us, even in our ordinary life, though we are not aware of it, a world in which we lived before descending into our physical being through birth or conception, as described the day before yesterday ; a world in which we shall live again when we pass through the portal of death, for then we shall recognise it as a world which belongs to us and which is not limited by birth and death. But there is one thing which rises up before us when we enter the spiritual world. We cannot enter this world in the same abstract theoretic manner with which we can live in the physical world and in the world of thoughts or of the intellect. In the physical world and in the world of thoughts we use ideas and thoughts, which as such, leave us cold. With a little self-observation anyone can discover that when he ascends to the sphere of pure thinking, when he surrenders to the external sensory world without any special interest or a close connection with it, the external physical world, as well as the world of ideas, really leaves him cold. We must learn to know this in detail from particular examples in life. We should note, for instance, how different are the inner feelings with which we consider our home, from those with which we look upon any other strange country which is indifferent to us. This will show us that in order to have a living interest for the environing world, our feeling and our will must first be drawn in through special circumstances. Feeling will indeed always dive down into the physical world when we awake, obtaining from this physical world a connection with the senses and the understanding. The fact that love or perhaps hate are kindled in us when we encounter certain people in the physical world, the fact that we feel induced to do certain things for them out of compassion, all this demands the inclusion of our feelings and of everything which constitutes our inner being, when we come across such things in the external physical world. How conscious we are of the fact that our inner life grows cold, when we rise up to spheres which are generally called the spheres of pale, dry thought and of theoretic study!

The being which lives in a dull twilight state from the moment of falling asleep to the moment of waking up, must, as it were, connect itself during the waking daytime condition with thoughts and with sensory experiences through an inner participation in these processes, thus giving rise to the whole wealth of interest in the external world.

And so we recognise that in life itself feeling and will must first be drawn into the sense world and into the world of thoughts. But we perceive this in the fullest meaning of the word only when through supersensible knowledge, we become free from the physical and etheric bodies, and have experiences outside them within our sentient-volitional being.

And hence it is evident that we must begin to speak of the world in a different way from how we speak in ordinary life, in ordinary consciousness. The dry ideas, the laws of Nature which we are accustomed to find in science and which interest us theoretically, though they leave us inwardly cold, these should be permeated with certain nuances and expressions which characterise the external world differently from the way in which we usually characterize it.

Our inner life acquires greater intensity through supersensible knowledge. We penetrate more intensively into the life of the external world. When we try to gain knowledge, we are then no longer able to submit coldly to inner ideas. No doubt one is then exposed to the reproach that the objectivity may suffer through a certain inner warmth, through the awakening of feeling and of a subjective sense. But this objection is only raised by those who are not acquainted with the circumstances.

The things perceived through supersensible knowledge make us speak differently of the supersensible objects of knowledge. These do not change, they do not become less objective, for in fact they are objective. When I look upon a wonderfully painted picture, it does not change through the fact that I look upon it with fire and enthusiasm; I should be a cold prosaic person if I were to face one of Raphael's Madonnas or one of Leonardo's paintings with a purely analytical artistic understanding, quite coldly and without any enthusiasm. It is the same when the spiritual worlds rise up in supersensible knowledge. Their content does not change through the fact that we connect ourselves with these worlds with inner feelings, far stronger than those which usually connect us with the external world and its objects.

When speaking from a knowledge of the higher worlds, many things will therefore have to be said differently, the descriptions will have to be different from those which we are accustomed to hear in ordinary life. But this does not render these worlds less objective. On the contrary, one could say: The subjective element which now breaks forth from the physical and etheric bodies becomes more objective, more selfless in its whole experience. And so the first experience which we have when going out of the physical body and experiencing our inner being consciously (whereas otherwise we always experience it unconsciously) is a feeling of absolute *loneliness*.

In our ordinary consciousness we never have the feeling that by dwelling only within our inner self, independently of anything in the world pertaining to us, complete loneliness fills our soul, that we ourselves, with everything which now constitutes our soul-spiritual content, must rely entirely upon ourselves.

The feeling of loneliness which sometimes arises in the physical world, but only as a reflection of the real feeling, though it is painful enough for many people, becomes immeasurably intensified when we thus penetrate into the supersensible world. But we then look back upon that which reflects itself as the spiritual environment in the mirror of the physical and etheric body which we left behind. We grow aware, on the one hand, of a complete feeling of loneliness, which alone enables us to maintain our Ego in this world . . . for we should melt away in this world of the spirit, if loneliness would not give us this Ego-feeling in the spiritual world, in the same way in which our body, our bodily sensation, gives us our Ego-feeling here on earth. To this loneliness we owe the maintenance of the Ego in the spiritual world. We then learn to know this spiritual world as our environment. But we know that we can only learn to know it through the inner soul-spiritual eye, even as we see the physical world through our physical eyes.

It is the same when the human being abandons his physical and etheric bodies by passing through the portal of death, and in this connection I shall enlarge the explanations already given yesterday. It is true that in this case the physical body is given over to the elements of the earth and that the etheric body dissolves, as I described, in the universal cosmic ether. But what we learned to know as our physical world, through our feeling and will, the world in which we experienced ourselves through the ordinary consciousness between birth and death, this world remains to man. The physical body filled with substance and the body of formative forces permeated by etheric forces, are laid aside with death, but what we experienced within them remains as a mirroring element.

From the spiritual world we look back through death, through which we have passed, into our last earthly life. Just because we have before us this last earthly life as a firm resistance which mirrors everything, just because of this, everything which surrounds us as we pass through the soul-spiritual world between death and a new birth, can also reflect itself. Through these experiences we perceive everything rising up in a far more intensive life than the one which we learned to know here in the physical world. And we first perceive as a soul-spiritual being everything with which we were in some way connected through our destiny, through our Karma. The people we loved, stand before us as souls. In our supersensible vision we see all that we experienced together with them.

Those who acquire spiritual, supersensible knowledge, already acquire imaginative vision here in the physical world, through everything which I described to you. Those who pass through the portal of death in the ordinary way, acquire this faculty, though it is somewhat different from spiritual vision on earth, they acquire it after having passed through the portal of death. From the sheaths of the physical and etheric bodies which were laid aside, emerges everything with which we were connected by destiny, or otherwise, in this earthly life—it undoubtedly arises in a different way when those whom we left behind still live on the earth, where the connection with them is more difficult, but when they follow us through death, this connection exists in the free, soul-spiritual life. Everything in our environment with which we were connected as human beings rises up before us. To supersensible knowledge, the fact that people (if I may now express myself in words of the ordinary consciousness) who belonged together here in the physical world find each other again in the soul-spiritual world, after having passed through the portal of death, is not a belief to be accepted as a vague premonition, but it is a certainty, a fact just as certain as the results of physics or chemistry. And this is in fact something which the spiritual science of Anthroposophy can add to the acquisitions of modern culture.

People have grown accustomed to a certain feeling of certainty through the gradual popularisation of a scientific consciousness. They strive to gain some knowledge of the supersensible worlds, but no longer in the form of the old presentiments handed down traditionally in the religious beliefs, for they have been trained to accept that certainty which the external world can offer. In regard to that which lies beyond birth and death the spiritual science of Anthroposophy seeks to pave the way to this same kind of certainty. It can really do this. Only those who tread the path already described, the path leading into the spiritual worlds, can carry the knowledge acquired in physics or chemistry further, out into the worlds which we enter when we pass through the portal of death.

Not everything of course, appears to us in this way when we look back upon our physical body through supersensible knowledge outside the body. There is one thing which then appears to us very enigmatic, and this enigma can show us best of all that the spiritual science of Anthroposophy does not translate the truths which it includes in its spheres of knowledge into a prosaic, dry rationalism. It leads us to spiritual vision, or by communicating its truth it speaks of things which can be perceived through spiritual vision. But in being led to spiritual vision, we do not lose full reverence towards the mysteries contained in the universe, towards everything in the universe which inspires reverence and which can now be clearly perceived, whereas otherwise they are at the most felt darkly. This enigmatic something which I mean and which appears to us, is that we now learn to know man's relationship with the earth, particularly his relationship with the physical mineral earth.

I have already explained to you from many different aspects how our web of thoughts, which is connected with the physical body, remains behind, and in addition to what has been described to you, in addition to what reflects itself and leads us to a knowledge of man's eternal being, we can also recognise the nature of this mirror itself which we have before us.

One might say: Even as in the physical world we face a mirror and in this mirror the environing world appears simultaneously with our own self, so in supersensible knowledge the spiritual world appears through this mirror. But just as we can touch the material mirror with its foil and investigate its composition, so we can also investigate this mirror of the supersensible—namely, our physical body and our etheric body—when we are outside with our real soul-spiritual being.

And there one can see that during his earthly life man constantly takes in substances from the external world, in order to grow and to sustain his whole life. We certainly absorb substances from the animal and vegetable kingdoms, but all these substances which we absorb from the animal and vegetable kingdoms also contain mineral substances. Plants contain mineral substances, for the plant builds itself up from mineral substances. By taking in vegetable nourishment we therefore build up our own body out of mineral substances.

By looking back upon our physical body from outside, we can now perceive the true significance of the mineral substances which we absorb. For now spiritual vision reveals something of which our ordinary consciousness has not the faintest inkling, namely the activity of thinking. We have, as you know, left behind our thinking. Our thoughts continue, as it were, to glimmer and to shine within the physical body. Thus we can now observe the effects of thoughts in the physical body from outside, as something objective. And we perceive that the effect of thoughts upon man's physical body is a dissolution of its physical substances, which fall asunder, as it were, into nothing.

I know that this apparently contradicts the law of the conservation of energy, but there is no time now to explain more fully its full harmony with this law. The nature of my subject obliges me to express myself in somewhat popular terms. But it is possible to understand that the purely mineral in man, what he bears within him as purely mineral substances, must be within him because it must be dissolved by his thoughts. For otherwise his thoughts could not exist—this is the condition for their existence—his thoughts could not exist if they did not dissolve mineral, earthly substances, a fact also revealed by the spiritual sciences of earlier times, based more on intuitive feeling. This dissolution, this destruction of physical substances constitutes the physical instrumentality of thinking.

When our sentient-volitional part, our true inner being, lives within the physical body and within the etheric body and is filled by the activity of thinking, we now learn to recognise that this activity takes its course through the fact that physical substance is continually destroyed. We now learn to recognise how our ordinary consciousness really arises. We are not conscious because forces of growth hold sway in us, forces which develop in the rest of the organism through nutrition. For in the same measure in which the forces of growth are active within us, thinking is dulled. When we wake up, thinking must, so to speak, have a free hand to dissolve physical substances, to eliminate them from the physical body. To the spiritual science of Anthroposophy, the nervous system appears as that organ which mediates this secretion of mineral-physical substances throughout the whole body. And in this secretion of the mineral-physical develops just that thought-activity which we ordinarily carry with us through the world.

You therefore see that the spiritual science of Anthroposophy not only enables us to recognise the eternal in man, but also to know of the way in which this eternal works within the physical body; that, for instance, thought can only exist through the fact that man continually develops within himself the mineral substances, that is, something dead.

And so we can say: If we learn to know man from this aspect, we also learn to know death from another aspect. Ordinarily death confronts us as the end of life, as a moment in life, as an experience in itself. But when we throw light upon man's physical and etheric body in this way we learn to know the gradual course of death, or the separation of physical-mineral substance,— for death in fact, is nothing but the complete liberator of man's mineral-physical substance— we learn to know the continuous secretion of a dead, corpse-like element within us.

We recognise that from birth onwards, we are really always dying and only when with the whole body we accomplish that which we ordinarily accomplish through the nervous system, in a small part of the body, only then do we die.

We therefore learn to contemplate the moment of death by seeing it on a small scale in the activity of thinking in the human organism. And throughout the whole time that we pass through after death, we can only look back upon our physical body because the following fact exists: Whenever a thought lights up within you during your ordinary life, this is always accompanied by the fact that physical matter is secreted in the physical body, in the same way in which, for instance, physical substance separates from a precipitated salt-solution. This lighting up of thought you owe as it were, to this opaqueness, to this separating off of physical mineral substances. Inasmuch as you abandon the physical body, there is summed up in a comparatively brief space of time what lives in the continual stream of your thoughts. You confront the fact that in death you see lighting up as if all at once that which slowly glimmered and shone throughout your whole earthly life, from birth to death.

And through this powerful impression, in which the life of thoughts illuminates the soul like a mighty flash of lightning, man acquires the memory of his physical lives on earth. The physical body may be cast off, the etheric body may dissolve completely in the universal ether, but through the fact that we obtain in one experience this powerful thought-impression (to mathematicians I might say : this thought-integral in comparison with thought-differentials, from birth to death), we always have before us, throughout the time after death, as a mirroring element, our physical life on earth, even though we have laid aside our physical and etheric parts. And this mirroring element reveals everything which we experience when the human beings with whom we were connected by destiny in love or in hate, gradually come up, when the spiritual Beings who live in the spiritual world and do not descend to the earth, whose company we also now share, rise up before us.

The spiritual investigator may state this with a calm conscience, for he knows that he does not speak on the foundation of illusionary pictures; he knows instead that to supersensible vision, when supersensible vision arises through the organ of the physical and etheric bodies which are now outside, these things are just as real, can be seen just as really as physical colours are ordinarily perceived through physical eyes, or physical sounds through physical ears.

This is how the evolution of humanity forms part of the evolution of the world. If we study the development of the world, for instance, the mineral life on earth, we understand why there should be mineral, earthly laws. They exist so that they might also exist within us, and thinking is therefore bound up with the earth. But in perceiving how the Beings who have bound their thinking with the earth emerge from that which produces their thought, we also learn to recognise how man in his true being lifts himself above the merely earthly. This is what connects the development of the world with the development of humanity and unites them.

We learn to know the human being and at the same time we learn to know the universe. If we learn to know man's physical body and its mineralisation through thinking, we also learn to know through man's physical body the lifeless mineralised earth. This created a foundation for a knowledge of the evolution of the world from its spiritual aspect also.

When we thus learn to know man's inner being, we can consider the development of the world in the light of the ordinary earthly experiences through which we have passed since our birth.

If you draw out of your memory-store an experience which you had ten years ago, a past event which you have gone through rises up before your soul as an image. You know exactly from the circumstances of life that it rises up as a picture. Yet this picture conveys a knowledge of something which really existed ten years ago.

How does this arise ? Through the fact that in your organism certain processes remained behind which now summon up the picture. Certain processes have remained behind in your organism and these summon up in you the picture enabling you to re-construct what you experienced ten years ago. But supersensible knowledge leads us deeper into man's inner nature. We can perceive, for instance, that the physical body becomes mineralised during the thinking process; we perceive this in the same way in which we learn to know some past experience of our earthly life through the traces which it left behind within us.

In the same way the development of the earth can be understood from the development of man ; through the activity of the mineral in man we learn to know the task of the mineral kingdom within the development of the earth. And if, as already set forth, we learn similarly to know (I can only mention this, for a detailed description would lead us too far) how the vegetable kingdom is connected with man, and how the animal kingdom is connected with him (for this too can be recognised), then the development of the world can be grasped by setting out from the human being.

And within the development of the world we can then see something which is again of the same importance to those who are interested in modern civilisation, as are the facts which I explained in connection with a knowledge of the human being, of the eternal inner kernel of man.

We know that modern civilisation has succeeded, at least up to a certain point, in so regarding man's relationship to the development of the world as to attach him to the evolution of the animals,—even though the corresponding theories, or the hypotheses, as some people say, still contain much that is unclear, requiring completion and modification. We follow the development of the simplest organic beings up to the higher animals, and if we continue this line of observation we come indeed to the point of placing man at the summit of animal development. One person does it in this way, and the other in that way, one more idealistically, and the other more materialistically in accordance with Darwin's theory of evolutionary descent, but methodically, it can hardly be denied that if we wish to study man's physical nature according to natural-scientific methods, we must rank him with the animal kingdom,—as has been done for some time.

We must investigate how his head has changed in comparison with the heads of the different animal-species; we must investigate his limbs, etc., and we thus obtain what is known as comparative anatomy, comparative morphology, comparative physiology, and we then also form concepts as to how man's physical form has gradually developed out of lower beings in the course of the world's evolution. But in so doing we always remain in the physical sphere. On the one hand people take it amiss to-day if the anthroposophical spiritual investigator speaks of the spiritual world as I have taken upon myself to do in this lecture; from many sides this is viewed as pure fantasy, and although many people believe that it is well-meant . . . they nevertheless look upon it as something visionary and fanciful.

Those who become acquainted to some extent with what I have described, those who at least try to understand it, will see that the preparations and preliminary conditions for it are just as serious as, for instance, the preparations for the study of mathematics, so that it is out of the question to speak of sailing into some sort of fanciful domain. But just as on the one hand people take it amiss if one describes the spiritual world as a real visible world, so they take it amiss on the other hand if in regard to man's physical development one fully accepts those who follow man's development Darwinistically, with a natural-scientific discipline, along the animal line of descent, as far as man. No speculations should enter the observations made in the physical sphere and all sorts of things sought for there, as is done for instance, to-day in Neo-vitalism. This is full of speculations; the old vitalism was also full of speculative elements. But whenever we consider the physical world, we must keep to the physical facts.

For this reason, the anthroposophical spiritual investigator who on the one hand ventures to speak in a certain way of the conditions after death and before birth, as I have done, does not consider it as a reproach (i.e. he is not affected by it) when people tell him that his description of the physical world is completely that of a modern natural scientist. He does not bring any dreams into the sphere which constitutes the physical world. Even though people may call him a materialist when he describes the physical world, this reproach does not touch him, because he strictly separates the spiritual world, which can only be observed with the aid of a spiritual method, from the physical-sensory world, which has to be observed with the orderly disciplined methods of modern natural science.

A serious spiritual-scientific investigator must therefore feel particularly hurt and pained at reproaches made to him with regard to certain followers of spiritual science who sometimes rebuke natural science out of a certain pride in their spiritual-scientific knowledge and out of their undoubtedly shallow knowledge of natural science. They think that they have the right to speak negatively of science and of scientific achievements but the spiritual investigator can only feel deeply hurt at their amateurish, dilettantish behaviour. This is however not in keeping with spiritual science. The spiritual science of Anthroposophy is characterised by the fact that it deals just as strictly and scientifically with the external physical world, as with the spiritual world, and vice versa.

With this preliminary condition, the anthroposophical spiritual investigator stands entirely upon the ground of strictest natural-scientific observation in regard to the study of the world's development, but at the same time he turns his gaze towards the soul-spiritual world. And even as he knows that not only a physical process is connected with man's individual embryonic origin in the physical world, but that a soul-spiritual element unites with the human embryo, with the human germ, so he also knows that in the whole development of the world—though to the physical body it appears as a tapestry of sensory objects, and though it manifests itself to the web of thoughts, i.e. to the etheric body, in laws of Nature—he also knows that the physical world is permeated and guided in its whole development by spiritual forces, under the sway of spiritual Beings, that can be known through the methods I have described.

The anthroposophical investigator therefore knows that when he contemplates the external physical world in the sense of genuine science, he comes to the right boundary, where he may then begin with his spiritual investigation.

If we have conscientiously traced evolutionary development through the animal kingdom up to man, as Darwin or other Darwinians or Haeckel did, and if we have gone into its scientific justification we can then continue this in a spiritual-scientific direction, after having reached the boundary to which we are led by natural science.

We now discover that *contemplation of the form* into which we penetrate through supersensible knowledge, shows us the whole *significance of forms*, as they appear in the kingdom of man on the one hand, and in the animal-kingdom on the other; we discover the whole significance of these forms.

Equipped with the knowledge supplied by supersensible research, we see how the animal (this is at least the case with most animals, and exceptions can be easily explained) stands upon the ground with its four limbs, how its spine is horizontal, parallel with the surface of the earth, and how in regard to the spine, the head develops in an entirely different position from that of man. We learn to know the animal's whole form, as it were, from within, as a complex of forces, and also in relationship with the whole universe. And we thus learn to make a comparison: We perceive the transformation, the metamorphosis in the human form, in the human being whom we see standing upon his two legs, at right angles, so to speak, with the animal's spine, with his own spine set vertically to the surface of the earth and his head developing in accordance with this position of the spine.

By penetrating into the inner art of Nature's creative process, we learn to distinguish the human form from the animal form; we recognise this by entering into the artistic creative process of the cosmos. And we penetrate into the development of the world by rising from otherwise abstact constructive thoughts to thoughts which are inwardly filled with life, which form themselves artistically in the spirit.

The important thing to be borne in mind is that when it seeks to know the development of the world, anthroposophical spiritual research changes from the abstract understanding ordinarily described—and justly so—as dry, prosaic, systematic thought, or combining thought, into more concrete, real thought. Not for the higher spiritual world, in which concepts must penetrate by the methods described, but for the physical world, the forms in world-development should first be grasped through a kind of artistic comprehension, which in addition develops upon the foundation of supersensible knowledge.

By thus indicating how science should change into art, we must of course encounter the objection raised by those who are accustomed to think in accordance with modern ideas: "But science must not become an art!" Now this can always be said, as a human requirement. People can say: Now I forbid the logic of the universe to become an art, for we only learn to know reality by linking up thought with thought and by thus approaching reality. Yes, if the world were as people imagine it to be, one could refuse to ascend to art, to an artistic comprehension of forms; but if the world is formed in such a way that it can only be comprehended through an artistic comprehension, it is necessary to advance to such an artistic comprehension. This is how matters stand. That is why those people who were earnestly seeking to grasp the organic in the world-development really came to an inner development of the thinking ordinarily looked upon as scientific thinking, they came to an artistic comprehension of the world. And as soon as we observe with an artistic-intuitive eye the development of the world, beginning with the point where the ordinary Darwinistic theory comes to a standstill, we perceive that man, grasped as a whole, cannot simply be looked upon by saying that once there were lower animals in the world, from which higher animals developed, that then still higher animals developed out of these, and so forth, until finally man arose.

If we study embryology in an unprejudiced way, it really contradicts this conception. Although modern scientists set up the fundamental law of biogenetics and compare embryology with phylogeny, they do not interpret rightly what appears outwardly even in human embryology, because they do not rise to this artistic comprehension of the world's development. If we observe in a human embryo how the limbs develop out of organs which at first have a stunted aspect, how everything is at first actually head, we already obtain the first elements of what is revealed by the artistic comprehension of the human form as I meant it. It is not possible to range the whole human being with the animals. One cannot say: The human being, such as he stands before us to-day, is a descendant of the whole animal species. No, this is not the case. Just those who penetrate with genuine scientific conscientiousness into scientific Darwinism and its modern description of the development of the world, will discover that through a higher understanding it is simply impossible to place man at the end, or at the summit of the animal-chain of development; they must instead study the human head as such, the head of the human beings. This human head alone descends from the whole animal kingdom. Though it may sound strange and paradoxical, the part which is generally considered as man's most perfect part, is a transformation from the animal kingdom.

Let us approach the human head with this idea and let us study it carefully. Observe with a certain morphological-artistic sense how the lower maxillary bones are transformed limbs, how also the upper maxillary bones are transformed limbs, how everything in the head is an enhanced development of the animal form; you will then recognise in the human head that upon a higher stage it reveals everything which has been developed in the animal under so many different forms. You will then also understand why it is so.

When you observe the animal, you can see that its head hangs upon one extremity of the spine and that in the typical animal it is entirely subjected to the law of gravity. Observe instead the human head, observe how the human being stands within the cosmos. The human head is set upon a spine which has a vertical direction. It rests upon the remaining body in such a way that the rest of man protects the head, as it were, against being subjected to the force of gravity alone. The human head is really something which rests upon the remaining organism with comparative independence. And we come to understand that through the fact that the human head is carried by the remaining body, it really travels along like a person using a coach; for it is the rest of the body which carries the human head through the world. The human head has its transformed limbs which have become shrivelled, as it were, and it is set upon the rest of the organism. This remaining organism is related to the human head in the same way in which the whole earth with its force of gravity is related to the animal. In regard to the head, the human being is "membered" into his whole remaining body in the same way in which the whole animal is "membered" into the earth.

We now begin to understand the human being through the development of the world. And if we proceed in this knowledge of the human form with an artistic sense and understanding, we finally comprehend how the human head is the continuation of the animal-series and how the remaining body of man developed later, out of the earth, and was attached to the human head. Only in this way we gradually learn to understand man's development.

If we go back into earlier times of the past, we can only transfer into these primordial epochs that part of man which lies at the foundation of his present head-development. We must not seek the development of his limbs or of his thorax in those early ages, for these developed later. But if we observe the development of the world by setting out, as I described, from the human being, if we observe it in the same way in which we look upon some past experience through memory, we find that the human being had already begun his development in the world at a time when our higher animals, for instance, did not as yet exist. There were however other animal forms present at that time from which the human head has developed, but the higher animals of to-day were not in existence.

We can therefore say : (let us now take a later epoch of the earth) In the further course of his development, man developed his head out of earlier animal-beings through the fact that his spiritual essence animated him. That is why he could bring his head to a higher stage of development. He then added his limbs, which developed out of the regular forces of the earth. The animals which followed, could only develop to the extent to which man had developed with the exclusion of his head. They began their development later, so that they have not come as far as the human development of the head; they remain connected with the earth, while the human being separates himself from it.

This proves that it has a real meaning to say : Man is organised into the development of the universe in such a way that while he is connected with the animal kingdom, he rises above it through his spiritual development. The animals which followed man in their development could only develop as much as man had developed in his limbs and thorax . . . the head remained stunted, because a longer time of development should have preceded it, such as that of man, in order that the real head might develop.

Through an artistic contemplation of the forms in the world's development, the conscientiously accepted Darwinistic theory is transformed, in so far as it is scientifically justified to-day. And we recognise that in the development of the world the human being has behind him a *longer time of development* than the animals,—that the animals develop as their chief form that part which man merely adds to his head. In this way man reaches the point of lifting one part of his being out of the force of gravity, whereas the animals are entirely subjected to it. Everything which constituted our head with its sense-organs, is raised above the force of gravity, so that it does not turn towards heavy ponderable matter, but towards the ether, which fills the sensory world. This is the case above all with the senses; we should see this, if we were to study them more closely. In this way, for instance, the human organ of hearing depends upon an etheric structure, not only upon the air structure.

Through all this, the human being forms part not only of the material world, of the ponderable physical world, but he forms part of the etheric outer world. Through the etheric world he perceives, for instance, what the light conjures up before him in the world of colours, etc., etc. Even through his external form he rises above heavy matter, up to the free ether, and for this reason we see the development of the world in a different way when we ascend from natural science to spiritual science.

But when we rise up to an artistic conception, we also perceive the activity of the soul-spiritual in man, and we must rise up to such a conception if we wish to understand the human being. We should, for instance, be able to say : In regard to his soul-spiritual, sentient-volitional being, we must speak of loneliness and of a life in common with others, as if these were theoretical concepts, as I described to-day ; we must rise up to the moral world and finally we come to the religious world. These worlds are interwoven and form a whole.

If we study the human being in accordance with a natural-scientific mentality and in the sense of modern civilisation, we find on the one hand the rigid scientific necessity of Nature into which the human being is also inserted, and on the other hand, we find that man can only be conscious of his dignity and can only say : I am truly man, if he can feel within him the moral-religious impulses. But if we honestly stand upon the foundation of natural science, we have pure hypotheses as to the beginning and the end of the earth, hypotheses which speak of the Kant-Laplace nebula for the beginning of the earth and of a heat-death for the end of the earth.

If in the face of the natural-scientific demands we now consider, in the sense of modern civilisation, the moral-religious world which reveals itself intuitively (I have shown this in my *Philosophy of Spiritual Activity*), if we consider this world we must say: We really delude ourselves, we conjure up before us a fog. Is it possible to believe that when the earth passes through the death by heat, that there should still exist anything else in the sense of natural science than the death too of all ideals?

At this point spiritual science, or Anthroposophy steps in, and shows that the soul-spiritual is a reality, that it is working upon the physical and that it has placed man in the human form, into the evolution of the world. It shows that we should look back upon animal-beings which are entirely different from the present animals, that it is possible to adhere to the methods of modern science, but that other results are obtained. Anthroposophy thus inserts the moral element into the science of religion, and Anthroposophy thus becomes moral-religious knowledge.

Now we no longer merely look towards the Kant-Laplace nebula, but we look at the same time to an original spiritual element, out of which the soul-spiritual world described in Anthroposophy has just as much developed as the physical world has developed out of a physical-earthly origin. And we also look towards the end of the earth and since the laws of entropy are fully justified, we can show that the earth will end through a kind of death by heat. But we look towards the end just as from the anthroposophical standpoint we can view the end of the single human being: his corpse is handed over to the elements, the human being himself passes over into a spiritual world. This is how we envisage the end of the earth. The scientific results do not disturb us, for we know that everything of a soul-spiritual nature which men have developed will pass through the earth's portal of death when the earth no longer exists; it will pass over into a new world-development, even as the human being passes over into a new world-development when he passes through death.

By surveying the development of the earth in this way, we perceive *in the middle of its development the event of Golgotha.* We see how this event of Golgotha is placed in the middle of the earth's development, because formerly, there only existed forces which would have led man to a kind of paralysis of his forces. We really learn to recognise (I can only allude to this at the end of my lecture) that in the same way in which through the vegetable and animal fertilization a special element enters the fertilised organism, so the Mystery of Golgotha brought something into the evolution of the world from spiritual worlds outside the earth, and this continues to live, it accompanies the souls, until at the end of the earth, they pass on to new metamorphoses of earthly life. I should have to describe whole volumes were I to show the path leading in a strictly conscientious scientific way from what I have described to you to-day in connection with the evolution of humanity and of the universe, to the mystery of Golgotha, to the appearance of the Christ-Being within earthly existence.

But through a spiritual-scientific deepening many passages in the Gospel will appear in an entirely new light, in a different way from what it has hitherto been possible for Western consciousness. Let us consider only the following fact: If we take our stand fully upon a natural-scientific foundation, we must envisage the physical end of the earth. And those who continue to stand upon this scientific foundation, will also find that finally the starry world surrounding the earth will fall away; they will look upon a future in which this earth below will no longer exist and the stars above will no longer exist. But spiritual science gives us the certainty that just as an eternal being goes out of the physical and etheric body every evening and returns into them every morning, so an eternal being will continue to live on when its individual body falls away. When the whole earth falls away from all the human soul-spiritual beings, this eternal part will continue to live and it will pass over to new planetary phases of world evolution.

Now Christ's words in the Gospels resound to us in a new and wonderful way: *Heaven and earth shall pass away, but My words shall not pass away*, and connected with these words are those of St. Paul: *Not I, but Christ in me*. If a Christian really grasps these words, if one who really understands Christianity inwardly and who says,

"Not I, but Christ in me," understands Christ's words, "Heaven and earth shall pass away, but My words shall not pass away," that is, what lives within my everlasting Being shall not pass away,—these words will shine forth from the Gospel in a remarkable way, with a magic that calls forth reverence, but if one is really honest they cannot be directly understood without further effort.

If we approach such words and others, with the aid of spiritual science and in the anthroposophical sense, if we approach many other sayings which come to us out of the spiritual darkness of the world-development, of the development of the earth and of humanity, a light will ray on to them. Indeed, it is as if light were to fall upon such words as "Heaven and earth shall pass away, but My words shall not pass away"—light falls upon them, if we hear them resounding from that region where the Mystery of Golgotha took place, that event through which the whole development of the earth first acquires its true meaning.

Thus we see that spiritual science in the sense of Anthroposophy strives above all after a conscientious observation of the strict methods of the physical world, but at the same time it seeks to continue these strict scientific methods into regions where our true eternal being shines out towards us, regions where also the spiritual being of the world-development rays out its light towards us, a light in which the world-development itself with its spiritual forces and Beings appears in its spiritual-divine character.

At the conclusion of my lecture let me express the following fact: Spiritual-scientific Anthroposophy can fully understand that modern humanity, particularly conscientious, scientifically-minded men, have grown accustomed to consider as real and certain the results of causal natural-scientific knowledge, the results of external sense-observation, intellectual combinations of these sensory observations, and experiments. And by acquiring this certainty, they acquired a certain feeling in general towards that which can be " certain." Up to now no attempt has been made to study supersensible things in the same way in which physical things are studied. This certainty could therefore not be carried into supersensible regions. To-day people still believe that they must halt with a mere faith at the threshhold of the supersensible worlds, that feelings full of reverence suffice, because otherwise they would lose the mystery, and the supersensible world would be rationalised. But spiritual science does not seek to rationalise the mystery, to dispel the reverent feeling which one has towards the mystery: it leads man to these mysteries through sight. Anthroposophy leaves the mystery its mystery-character, but it sets it into the evolution of the world in the same way in which sensory things exist in the sphere of world-evolution.

And it must be true that men also need certainty for the spheres transcending mere Nature. To the extent in which they will feel that through spiritual science in the sense of Anthroposophy they do not hear some vague amateurish and indistinct talk about the spiritual worlds, but something which is filled by the same spirit which comes to expression in modern science, to this same extent humanity will also feel that the certainty which it acquired, the certainty which it is accustomed to have through the physical world, can also be led over into the spiritual worlds. People will feel : If certainty exists only in regard to the physical world, of what use is this certainty, since the physical world passes away ? Man needs an eternal element, for he himself wants to be rooted in an eternal element. He cannot admit that this certainty should only be valid for the transient, perishable world. Certainty, the certainty of knowledge, must also be gained in regard to the imperishable world.

This is the aim pursued in greatest modesty (those who follow the spiritual science of Anthroposophy know this) by Anthroposophy. Its aim is that through his natural certainty man should not lose his knowledge of the imperishable ; through his certainty in regard to perishable things he should not lose the certainty in regard to imperishable things. Certainty in regard to the imperishable, that is to say, certainty in regard to the riddle of birth and death, the riddle of immortality, the riddle of the spiritual world-evolutions, this is what Anthroposophy seeks to bring into our civilisation.

Anthroposophy believes that this can be its contribution to modern civilisation. For in the same measure in which people courageously recognise that certainty must be gained also in regard to imperishable things, and not only in regard to perishable things, in the same measure they will grow accustomed to look upon Anthroposophy no longer as something fantastic and as an idle individual hobby, but as something which must enter our whole spiritual culture, like all the other branches of science, and thereby our civilisation in general.

JESUS OR CHRIST

Here in Norway I naturally feel that I am a guest, and I must above all express my heartfelt thanks, both to the speaker who has just addressed to me such warm words, and to all of you who have shown your interest by coming to hear what I have to say, in the short space of time at my disposal, concerning the problem indicated in our subject. I should like to say in advance, my dear friends, that I feel myself in a double sense a guest within the Theological Movement, for the reason that, in the Anthroposophical Movement, I have always emphasised the fact that Anthroposophy does not in any way wish to be some sort of a new religious institution, or even a new sect, but that its aim is to grow out of the modern scientific movement in general. Anthroposophy strives to find the suitable methods of investigation for the supersensible facts of human life and of universal existence. And, only in so far as the sphere of theology forms part of the general sphere of investigation, does Anthroposophy feel inclined—if asked—to contribute to theological investigation what it believes to be able to give in this direction with the aid of methods belonging to a supersensible investigation. It was for this reason that, when a large number of young theologians approached me in Germany, I said that I was willing to help them only with what I could offer from an Anthroposophical standpoint; for whatever is needed to-day within the theological religious movement itself must be undertaken by persons who stand within this theological or religious life.

The chief objection raised against Anthroposophy from this direction is that it strives, with the aid of its methods of investigation, to rise through the acquirement of knowledge into supersensible worlds—that it strives to develop certain latent cognitive faculties in man, in order to penetrate into supersensible worlds and investigate them. The objection is raised, in these same theological circles, that this is really in contradiction to the religious spirit—to religious piety—and that this is the very thing, therefore, which must be rejected by Christian theology. And this has recently been expressed especially clearly by saying that religion must work with the irrational, with the mystery that must not be unveiled through rationalism. Religion should work with an element that does not wish to be understood, but should rather be venerated, with the deepest and most trustful reverence, as an impenetrable mystery. It has even been stated that Christianity makes use of paradox, in order to draw out and to form the truly Christian religious life with sufficient depth, out of direct human trustfulness.

If Anthroposophy were to strive to rationalise the irrational, especially in connection with the problem of Christ-Jesus, and to draw down into the regions of cold understanding what is contained in the Mystery of Golgotha, the objections raised from this direction would in that case be justified. Moreover, these objections are supplemented by still another one. Since Anthroposophy is not Gnosticism, nor mysticism, nor a non-historical orientalism, it takes into account absolutely the historical development in human evolution. Gnosticism is non-historical, mysticism is non-historical, all oriental world-conceptions are in a certain sense non-historical. Anthroposophy is a western world-conception, through and through, particularly as regards its historical standpoint; and it considers historical evolution as something real— just as one is accustomed to do, in the scientific life of the West. Anthroposophy feels compelled, therefore, to place the personality of Jesus within the historical life of humanity. It knows what this historical Jesus bore within Himself, for humanity; only it is compelled, for reasons which I wish to explain to-day, to ascend from the man Jesus, who can be observed in his earthly life, to the super-terrestrial, extra-terrestrial, cosmic Being of the Christ, who incarnated in the man Jesus; so that Anthroposophy can really speak, in a certain sense, of Christ-Jesus as a twofold Being.

The objection may be raised at this point, that what Anthroposophy has to say about the cosmic, or even about the telluric Christ, has really no importance whatever, for the religious life of modern humanity. Modern humanity, it will be said, wishes to limit its contemplation to earthly facts, when considering historical evolution, so that there is no longer any need to place the cosmic Christ beside the historical Jesus.

Now, my dear friends, the first thing which I shall have to show you is the way in which Anthroposophy must face the facts of the world and how it attains to a quite special attitude toward this Mystery of Golgotha through its methods of research.

Anthroposophy strives, in the first place, to grasp in a quite definite way, devoid of illusion and in quite clear outlines, what has developed in western humanity—especially since the middle of the fifteenth century—as that form of knowledge, which I may call the "knowledge of physical objects". Through this form of knowledge, the world of Nature has already been explained, systematised and grasped, in accordance with its laws, in a truly wonderful way, (indeed, the ideal of science, quite justifiably, has even more extensive aims than this); and we have a subjective parallel phenomenon in a sound and dignified science, the fact that man becomes rationalistic—I might even say abstract—in the acquirement of knowledge. The world of thought acquires more and more this character of mere pictures. If we go back beyond the fifteenth century, we shall find that the world of thought did not possess at that time the character of pictures, or that abstract character which merely *designates* Reality, but does not contain it—that same character which the world of thought has acquired ever since the fifteenth century, and particularly since the time of Galileo and Giordano Bruno. Ideas, for us to-day, signify at the most the image of Reality. If we go back beyond the fifteenth century, we find that man did not as yet feel that a true spiritual Reality enters his being, when he surrenders himself to the world of thought. At that time man possessed, not only the abstract world of ideas, but a world of ideas filled with Spirit,—really permeated by Spirit.

As far as rationalism and natural science are concerned, great and wonderful results have been achieved, during recent centuries. And we come to see, more and more clearly, how also other sciences, such as the science of history, have become affected by the mentality and the manner of thinking which rules in those fields. One who follows the change that has taken place in the methods of investigation during recent centuries—as this affects the sphere of theology—will find that the mentality in these investigations was influenced throughout by the natural-scientific direction of thought, for history has, in fact, in modern times, assumed the characteristic of a natural-scientific mentality.

Thus, Christology has gradually become a historical "investigation of the life of Jesus". This is quite comprehensible, when we look upon the whole course of spiritual evolution in modern times. We must understand that this has to be so. But we must also understand that this direction, if followed further, will tend at the same time to rob Christianity of the Christ, and will approach more and more closely to what can be offered by the neutral attitude toward religion of a historian like Ranke, for instance, who placed the personality of Jesus within the historical course of events, as the noblest Being who ever walked upon earth.

Theology has thus approached even nearer to historical investigation—until, to-day, we find that many theologians can hardly be distinguished, in their mentality and methods of investigation, from a historian as eminent as Ranke.

In contrast to this, Anthroposophy emphasises that certain cognitive forces which remain latent in man during ordinary life, and are also latent in ordinary science—forces of which we are not conscious, but which are nevertheless contained in every man and can be drawn up out of his consciousness—lead man through knowledge out of the mere sense-world and enable him to grasp by its means a supersensible world, in the same way that a human being, endowed with senses, is able to grasp the sense world.

An attitude and a method such as this—which is no longer connected with mere physical objects, and which possesses nothing of the ordinary form of rationalism, but rather comes ever nearer to knowing true experience—enables man, through his own efforts, to approach the supersensible world.

Now, it is an error which one frequently encounters, to believe that Anthroposophy seeks to transfer to a supersensible sphere the characteristics belonging to knowledge gained in the sphere of science or rationalism; that Anthroposophy accordingly is itself a rational thing, and therefore obliterates mystery and everything which is irrational, or paradox and requires a logical acceptance of what it looks upon as the mystery of Golgotha—at the same time, not an acceptance based upon confidence and reverence that is freely given, as is required by Religion. Yet the whole picture of the world and of man himself changes completely when we ascend beyond the scientific or historical sphere of knowledge, and arrive at the knowledge of the supersensible sphere—if I may uses this expression. I can merely allude to such things on this occassion, but if we wish to trace the most characteristic aspect of the ordinary scientific method, limited to physical objects and recognised at the present time, it is this: that for one who really and honestly draws the last possible conclusion from natural science and rationalism, it divides the world into two spheres. These two spheres will not always be noticed, because there is present in man a certain inner and unconscious fear of drawing these ultimate conclusions. Nevertheless, anyone who has learned to know, as I have done, human beings who have suffered deeply because of this twofold division in human nature, and who have drawn, with all the fervour of their hearts and their religious feeling, the very last conclusions possible in modern thought; anyone who has seen the great suffering of souls, the groping without direction which may be found attaching itself, just in connection with the deepest religious feeling, to this dualism in modern rationalistic science and to its attitude toward man, will feel inclined to reflect and to consider how it was that dualism gave rise to a cognitive attitude also in the religious sphere. For natural science does indeed exert too great a power upon the human mind. In the face of its conceptions, man's responsibility is so great that he must strive to shape other scientific methods according to the model of the natural-scientific, historical, realistic method.

But where does this method lead to, if it is to draw the ultimate conclusions? It leads to where a deep abyss—an abyss which cannot be bridged by a knowledge limited to physical objects—arises between what we acknowledge as natural-scientific necessity and what we grasp within our moral-ethical life: what ultimately guarantees our true human dignity. And if we truly experience this moral-ethical life, it will appear to us as the direct outflow of the Divine, leading us unswervingly toward religious piety—toward religiosity. At the same time, this deep abyss between ethical-religious life and what natural science reveals, as far as physical man is concerned, may indeed be concealed from man's view by a veil of mist, owing to a certain inner unconscious sphere. Yet anyone who tries with absolute honesty to understand human nature, will find that this contrast cannot be bridged with the aid of natural science.

A hypothesis fully justified from a scientific standpoint—the Kant-Laplace theory—is applied to the beginning and to the end of earthly existence. I will refrain from speaking about this in detail, for—although this theory has now been modified—it stands there, nevertheless, as something, at the beginning of the world, which is quite indifferent to human evolution as the source of those ethical-divine ideals to which we surrender ourselves as to something, the existence of which cannot be questioned, yet something which exists merely in the form of images or pictures. Again, if we also contemplate the end of earthly existence from a natural-scientific aspect, we find another hypothesis, likewise justified from a scientific aspect—namely, the entropy theory, which speaks of death through heat, at the end of our earthly existence. Thus, a natural-scientific necessity places man between the Kant-Laplace nebula, and death through heat. Man lives between these two extremes, and surrenders himself to his ethical-religious ideals; nevertheless, ultimately he finds these unmasked as mere illusions, since, at the end of earthly existence, there faces him death through heat, and the immense corpse will swallow up, not only the physical-etheric elements contained in earth evolution, but also everything contained in ethical ideals.

My dear friends, it is most certainly not out of a religious rationalism, but out of a knowledge which I have gained in an elemental-cognitive way, that I am compelled to include in what is hidden by a veil of mist, by which we try to conceal what approaches man, and which can be one of the most painful of all soul-experiences, the fact that man has sought for information that did not exist in ancient religions, nor in the early times of Christian evolution—he has tried, namely, to distinguish between knowledge and faith. For knowledge, in spite of everything, gradually becomes a Moloch, owing to the power which it necessarily exercises over the human mind; and this Moloch gradually devours faith, if faith cannot cling to a higher, truly supersensible knowledge, which is able to approach even the Mystery of Golgotha.

And here it is that Anthroposophy must draw attention to the fact that what is supplied by a rigid, natural-scientific necessity will assume, for supersensible knowledge, merely the form of a phenomenon—just as the world which we see with our eyes, and hear with our ears, dissolves into phenomenalism. I can merely allude to these things to-day, but Anthroposophy tries to show that what we see with our eyes has nothing to do with the material world, but with the world of phenomena. And, in supersensible knowledge, the sense-world loses something of its rigid solidity, as it were; while, on the other hand, the ethical-religious world loses likewise some of its abstractness, some of its estrangement from physical necessity. The two worlds draw nearer to each other. The ethical-religious world becomes more real, and the physical sense-world assumes more of the nature of phenomena. And it is not through speculation, not through an abstract philosophical method, but through real experience, that a world is built up which transcends our ordinary sense-world. Moreover, this world, which we then see, no longer contains any contrast between what is ideal and what is real. Both have drawn nearer together. The laws of Nature become moral—I might say—in this other world, and the moral laws are condensed into events of Nature. Let me mention only this one fact: Anthroposophy also, to be sure, places something resembling death through heat at the end of earthly existence, but Anthroposophy considers that what man bears within him as moral, religious ideals, is like a seed for a future existence—just as the life of this year's plants passes on, through seeds, into the plant-life of next year. Anthroposophy here collides strongly with a certain paradox contained in modern science—after all, I do not hesitate to say this here, because I believe that it will meet with less objection in a circle of theologians than in a circle of rigid natural scientists: I shall venture to say, namely, that Anthroposophical spiritual knowledge knows that the so-called law of the conservation of energy and of matter is no longer valid in a world which is described as a supersensible world: and it also knows that this law of the conservation of energy and of matter has a merely relative validity in the world which appears as the world Nature, and is comprehended by rationalism.

Anthroposophy teaches us to realize—in the

case of the human organism—that it is not matter alone that is to be found transforming itself there, that it is not only metamorphosis of matter that takes place. Outside the human organism, in the rest of the world of Nature, the laws of the conservation of energy and of matter hold good. Within the human being himself, however, Anthroposophy teaches us that there is a complete disappearance and overcoming of matter, and that a resurrection of new matter takes place, arising out of mere space. If I were to use a trivial comparison, in order to point out the situation with regard to matter and energy in the human organism, I should express myself as follows: in our study of the law of the conservation of energy and of matter, we miss the road in the same way that someone else might do, who said that he had counted exactly how many bank-notes had been deposited in the bank during a certain period of time, and how many had been taken out again; and that he had found that exactly the same number had been deposited as had been taken out.

We see that just as much energy passes into matter, as is given out again. Nevertheless, in the same way that we may not draw the conclusion that things in the bank remain unchanged, but must admit that independent work has to be carried on there—indeed, that the bank-notes may even be reprinted and then given out again in a completely new form—so in the case of the human organism we may not draw such conclusions as are formed in connection with the law of the conservation of matter and of energy. Both the *destruction* of matter and energy and the *creation* of matter and energy take place.

This is not the product of some irresponsible fantasy; on the contrary, it is something which finds absolute recognition within the sphere of exact Anthroposophical investigation. As far as the outer world is concerned, it is true that the law of the conservation of matter and energy holds good—that is to say, for the *middle* stage of evolution. When we approach the *end of the earth,* however, (and we accept, with a certain justification, the theory of consumption of the earth by fire) we do not see an enormous grave-yard, but we find that everything which has been developed by man, in the way of moral and aesthetic ideals and godlike, spiritual convictions, can indeed unite itself, within man, with the new forms of matter that will have arisen, and that, in consequence of this, we have to do with an actual seed of continuing development. Through that which arises in man, the death of external matter will be overcome.

We find, in Anthroposophical Spiritual Science, something which does indeed show us that ethical and moral forces also, are directly active within matter. In the case of man, this remains, for ordinary consciousness at the present time, in the unconscious. But, to repeat: for that stage of consciousness which is reached in Anthroposophical investigation, we must recognise absolutely, that what is ethical, moral and religious is condensed to reality, and that whatever lives in the external world of matter dissolves into a mere sequence of phenomena. Thus, the two worlds come nearer toward each other. Moreover, we shall also then find them coming nearer together, when we see just how things look to the human being who lives in this higher knowledge. We are accustomed to speak and to judge logically, when we apply ordinary rationalism to the outer world of Nature and base our standpoint upon logical categories of this sort, which are quite justifiable for the outer sense world. Anthroposophical Spiritual Science deviates also from this method simply out of objective necessity. It must deviate from it, because with its methods of knowledge, it not only experiences, but also observes things differently.

There are two concepts, in particular, which manifest themselves. (There are many others, besides these, to be sure, which also manifest themselves, but these two must be considered especially important for us to-day.) There are two concepts which we otherwise know only indirectly as objects, but which we do not ordinarily apply in the way in which we apply logical concepts. For, in the world of true knowledge, even that becomes expression, becomes revelation, is brought nearer to reality, which otherwise remains formal, ideal.

The two concepts which here appear to us are the concepts of illness and health. You will all admit, my dear friends, that, from the standpoint of logical categories in the ordinary sens-world, it is quite impossible to speak of "healthy" and "ill"—to speak of what is not only true, but what is acknowledged because it is *healthy*. In the world of organic Nature, we recognise whatever is healthy as the principle of growth and development; we recognise what is ill as deformity, as an impediment to normal development. When we employ logical categories however, we do not speak of healthy and ill. When we progress from the ordinary knowledge of external objects to that knowledge which is applied by Anthroposophical Spiritual Science, we must begin to speak in terms of *healthy* and *ill*. For our observation compels us to find, in the supersensible world into which we now enter, not any longer ideas and concepts, but *experiences* (*healthy* and *ill* are experiences!).

What we designate in the sense-world with the mere abstraction "true", must be replaced by "healthy" in the supersensible world. And what we designate in the sense-world as "untrue", "wrong", must be replaced by "ill", when experienced in the supersensible world.

And here the possibility presents itself for Anthroposophy—not through any wish to approach it by force, but through an entirely honest and straightforward pursuit of the investigation itself—to connect the investigation of the immediate present with the Old and New Testaments. Moreover, the cleft between modern investigation and the Old and New Testaments is here actually bridged. A new path to an understanding of the

Mystery of Golgotha is here opened up. For something presents itself here which is very paradoxical.... As I have already said, I can refer to these matters only more or less in outline to-day; nevertheless, what I shall thus present to you in a rough sketch is the result of investigation, carried on throughout many years—investigation which did not proceed out of any religious prejudice, if I may be permitted to use these words. I myself started out with an absolutely natural-scientific education; having grown up in my youth with the greatest imaginable spiritual freedom. I brought no religious feelings over with me from my youth. Through investigations, and as the ultimate consequences of my natural-scientific investigations, I have been finally impelled to say what I believe I now have the right to say, from an Anthroposophical point of view, even concerning the origin of religious problems. Thus prejudices, even subjective ones, really do not come into question here. But, through Anthroposophical investigations, we first recognise that we have the world of Nature round about us, particularly if our understanding of Nature is in complete accordance with the methods and significance of natural science, through which we can really learn to know Nature more accurately (even though, of course, this will not always be admitted, and natural science often is contaminated, as it were, by all sorts of mysticism). If we really understand Nature, not only with regard to its phenomena and its laws, but also through the fact that we can form certain conceptual ideas concerning what it really is, we shall then say to ourselves: whatever takes places, out there in Nature, continues its course also in man. Whatever takes place outside the human skin, is also to be found inside the skin of the human being standing before use. We find processes of Nature outside and we find them also inside, within us. But here we come upon the paradox which reveals itself to Anthroposophical investigation: namely, that all ascending processes of Nature, in man—all those processes which strive toward fruitfulness—have only a limited period of validity, and become within man tearing-down, destructive processes.

And as a result of a manifold observation of Nature and of innumerable Anthroposophical studies of the human being, this forceful and overpowering thought comes to us: Nature is permitted to be Nature outside the boundaries of the human skin; inside the sheath of man's skin, however, whatever was Nature becomes the very opposite of Nature.

If, now, we have risen to the height of supersensible methods of research we see that the forces which are constructive forces in Nature, become destructive forces in man, and that these destructive forces in man's nature become the bearers of evil. This is the difference which Anthroposophy must point out, in contrast to mere idealism: that Nature is permitted to remain Nature, whereas man's inner life is not permitted even in the sphere of the body to remain Nature. Even from the aspect of Nature, whatever is active in man as a continuation of Nature becomes something pathological, and hence, something evil. Nature, outside of us, is neutral toward good and evil; *in* us, its activity is destructive—conducive to illness and evil, even from the bodily aspect. Moreover, we are able to withstand whatever is active in us as evil—and this again can be seen through Anthroposophical perception—only through the fact that during life between birth and death, our contact with external Nature is such as to permit our life to become only a reflexion of external Nature; we do not grasp with our consciousness what is organically active in the depths of our human nature, as primal foundation of evil. We fill our consciousness by receiving sense-perceptions from outside; we receive these exterior sense-impressions, but we convey them only to a certain point—beyond this, they may not go; for, if they did so, (supersensible knowledge shows us this) they would poison us, as it were. We reflect them back.

In consequence of this, a boundary line arises between all that constitutes the organs of consciousness in man—those organs which receive external Nature—and all that constitutes the continuation of Nature itself, the further development of its constructive forces in man. The conscious processes do not reach beyond this boundary line, but are instead reflected back, and form our memory or power of recollection. What lives in our memory, is reflected external Nature, which does not penetrate into us any more deeply than a ray of light into a mirror. For if man were to become conscious of what lies concealed behind his inner mirror, of what lies in those depths where Nature becomes evil in him, he himself would become an evil being, through this activity of Nature in him.

On the other hand, if we limit ourselves to these reflected pictures, to memories, to the mere reflexion of Nature outside of us, there would be one thing to which we could not attain: namely, to a full Ego-consciousness, a self-contained Ego-consciousness. We should not be able to attain to this. What we are accustomed to sum up as self-consciousness, what lives in our consciousness as Ego, can arise only out of our bodily nature—its primal roots are grounded in the Nature of man. For this reason, rationalism, for its part, is just as neutral in its attitude toward good and evil as are the laws of nature. Yet, if all that constitutes human self-consciousness were to extend over the other side of man's soul-life, this awakening of the Ego during the present period of human evolution would bring about an irresistible inclination to evil—to that which lives in us as destructive forces of Nature.

At this point there now arises a significant contribution to knowledge, which leads us over into the sphere of religion (this may be seen, particularly if the physical world is contemplated from a supersensible point of view). When the human being surrenders himself completely to everything that constitutes the working of Nature, to the forces that permeate natural phenomena, he comes to the point where he says that Atheism is not only logically incorrect, but that it is in fact an illness. It is not an illness which is ordinarily detected, but Anthroposophical Spiritual Science, for the very reason that it substitutes, from its supersensible point of view, the concepts "healthy" and "ill" for the simple concepts "correct" and "incorrect", is in a position to say that in these combinations of fluids in man, which are no longer familiar to external physiology and biology, there is present something pathological, when a human being declares, with all the conviction of his soul, that there is no God. For a man with a sound and healthy nature says, in spite of the fact that he is capable of doing evil—this evil remains in the subconsciousness—a sound and healthy human nature says, "there *is* a God."

At the same time, this consciousness that there is a God, which is the immediate expressioin of a genuine human healthiness, contains only that acknowledgment of God which I might call the acknowledgment of the Father. We can do no more by submerging ourselves in Nature, by experiencing Nature within us, than to attain to the *consciousness of the Father*.

Anyone, therefore, who remains rooted in modern natural science can attain only to the consciousness of the Father; and he will more or less lose the Son, *the consciousness of the Christ,* from out of the ranks of Divine Beings, even though he will not admit this. The fundamental character of

Harnack's book, "Wesen des Christentums", (Essence of Christianity) is contained in its statement that the Son really has no place in the Gospels, but only the Father; for the Son is merely the One Who sent out into the world the teachings of the Father, by way of the Gospels.

The preceding conception actually leads us gradually away from a real or true Christianity, for, if we wish to preserve Christianity, we must be able to add to the distinct and separate experience of the Father—which we attain to, if we really possess a sound human nature—the *experience of the Son*. But this experience of the Son is the very one which arises, not through an experience of Nature, but through the experience of something in man which transcends Nature. It is an experience belonging to that sphere which has nothing in common with Nature, in contrast to which Nature fades away into mere phenomenalism. And then there arises the possibility that the experience of the Son may be added to the experience of the Father.

Just as the experience of the Father is simply the result of perfect, harmonious health, so the experience of the Son is a fact which we pass through, in our inner life, when we begin to notice that we are rising to the full consciousness of our Ego; that we must develop this Ego during our life on earth, and that this Ego-consciousness is itself absolutely connected with Nature. If we do not wish that it should become a prey to evil, then this awakening of the Ego must attain, during the course of our life on earth, to where it becomes permeated with the divine spiritual content. The words, "Not I, but Christ in me", must become truth.

It must become truth, for the reason that the Ego—which can remain within the Father experience, in the form in which it is first experience—must be completely transformed and metamorphosed.

Man need not become ill through what is merely the reflection of outer Nature, when the latter does not itself enter his consciousness, but appears merely in mirrored pictures, in reflexions; but man would of necessity become ill, as regards his true human Being, were he unable to find, out of his own freedom, that World-power which is not limited to being only the primal origin of what exists as healthy forces of Nature. The human being must be able to lift himself to the recognition that this process of becoming ill must inevitably take place through the birth of the Ego. The rest of man's soul-life might, under certain circumstances, remain healthy; but the stability of the Ego would, nevertheless, of necessity cause this soul-life to become ill, if the human being were not able to meet, during his life, in an inward, sense-free experience, that Being who can be found here upon the earth, yet who is Himself not of earth—who can be found only through the free act of the soul, and the finding of whom is therefore entirely different from the finding of the Father.

In western Europe little emphasis is laid upon

the distinction between these two experiences, the Father-experience and the Son-experience. On the other hand, if, in our day we turn to the East, and study, for example, such a work as the Philosophy of the Russian philosopher. Soloviev, we shall find, just in his case that he actually speaks like a man of the first Christian centuries, except that he clothes what he has to say out of this attitude of mind in modern philosophical formulas. We can see clearly from the way in which he speaks, that his experience of the Father is quite distinct from his experience of the Son. He experiences, instinctively, what we again must discover and acknowledge, through spiritual investigation: namely, that we are born out of the Father; that it is a sign of illnes not to acknowledge the Father; yet, at the same time, that for human beings endowed with an Ego, there must be a process that heals—a super-earthly Healer—and this is the Christ. Not to experience the Father means to be inwardly ill; not to experience the Christ means the entrance of sorrow and misfortune in our lives. The Father-problem is a question of knowledge. The Son-problem is a question of destiny—a question of blessing and misfortune. And only those epochs which have considered the Christ as a physician, as a universal Healer, have been able to attain to a satisfying conception of the way in which He enters our life. For supersensible Anthroposophical investigation, it is no mere phrase, not something which has a merely allegorical and symbolic meaning, when we say:

Christ the Physician, Christ the Saviour, or Healer (Heiland oder Heiler), He who sets the Ego free from that danger, from which the Father cannot free it—for whatever is healthy can also become ill. Through the Egoconsciousness alone, healthiness would necessarily disappear. What the Father is unable to do, He has conferred upon the Son. The Christ enters human consciousness. through a quite distinct experience, at the side of the Father.

Spiritual scientific Anthroposophical investigation can justify this experience in accordance with absolutely scientific methods. But, first, at this point, something would reveal itself, which I should like to call: *the eternally-present Christ.* We find Him if we only seek deeply enough, in our soul's being; we find Him as a Being whom we cannot bring forth out of our own soul. We find Him, as we find an external event of Nature outside of us—quite objectively. We meet Him after our birth, during the course of our human development. We must draw Him forth out of our moral perception. Yet, at the same time, He is the eternally-present Christ.

If, on the other hand, we have found this eternally-present Christ, if we have justified Him in the face of Anthroposophical investigation, we enter also upon historical investigation in a way quite different from the one we have previously followed. For this is the strange thing about it: that, when we ascend to the higher consciousness, we must first again descend to the ordinary consciousness. We cannot investigate the sense-world in a higher consciousnes. This would lead only to phrases and idle words. If someone were to develop a higher consciousness only—to know only what Anthroposophy is, he would have to beware of speaking about natural science; for he who wishes to speak about natural science must also have a thorough scientific knowledge of Nature, in accordance with the methods of modern investigation. He can, at the same time, permeate what natural science has to give, with supersensible investigation. A layman, a dilettante, is not permitted to speak on natural science, no matter how much at home he may be in the knowledge of the supersensible worlds. The supersensible worlds have, as a matter of fact, exactly the same significance for the sense-worlds which oxygen has, when it is outside the lungs. The lung is what corresponds to Nature. Spiritual science must first be poured into natural science, if natural science is to be made fruitful.

But here another sphere may be considered—and again I repeat, this is not because of any religious prejudice. One may approach it, at first, without any historical consideration, and quite without any help from the Gospels. It is what I should like to describe as that epoch of human development which coincides outwardly for us, with the Mystery of Golgotha.

It is a fact, that also one who does not advance to supersensible concepts and ideas may approach the Mystery of Golgotha. In this case, he will be tempted to proceed more and more in a purely external, naturalistic-historical way, and to transform Christ-Jesus into the simple personality of Jesus of Nazareth.

He who progresses to Anthroposophical spiritual investigation, finds everywhere the necessity, first of all, to permeate with knowledge everything that presents itself in the field of Nature and of ordinary history. It is only when approaching the historical Mystery of Golgotha, that he does not find this necessity. For, here, the higher concepts may be applied directly and without preconception. It is possible to comprehend directly, through supersensible investigation, what took place in the sense-world in just the way in which it took place.

Here we come to the next point. We see, now, that the Ego-development, about which I have already spoken to you, was actually not always present, in human development. We find justification, for example, for the fact that, the farther back we go in the evolution of speech, the more we find that the designation for "I", the Ego, is included within the *verb*— that the designation of the Ego, as a word by itself, appears only later in human evolution. Yet this is only something external. One who studies the psychology of history, while at the same time penetrating into it with supersensible perception, will find that the Ego-experience actually did not exist until about the eighth, or the seventh century before Christ; that it then gradually began to appear: and that historical development, in human history, actually tended toward what we must call the dawning of the Ego.

I believe it was especially in the life of the Greek people that the dawn of this Ego was felt so completely. This was not only because they were conscious of the fact that this Ego had its origin in Nature, and is therefore subjected to Nature—thus bringing death to man, if it develops for itself alone. For this reason, the Greeks really felt that it is better to be a beggar in the upper world, than a king in the world of Shades—this was an altogether justified feeling. But it was felt also in another way. He who really studies the great Greek dramatists—not in the superficial manner in which this is often done to-day—knows that they desired, at the same time, to be physicians; that they wished to shape the course of the drama in such a way that the human being might recover his health through a Katharsis. The Greeks had a sense for the need of healing, in their art.

And now if we pass over in this period of historical development into the Roman world, we feel how the content of the human soul—in religious life, in the life of the State, and in public life—becomes stiffened in abstract concept. We find humanity in great danger at that time, of becoming ill as a result of Ego-development. And we feel what it really means (I am not making use of analogy, nor playing with words, even if it may appear to be so—what I am saying is really the result of Anthroposophical investigation), we have a feeling for what it really means when, in the Orient, the

"Therapeutists" appeared—a certain Order which set itself the task of actually healing humanity, which was falling into illness, restoring it to health.

What we see arising in the course of historical evolution is that humanity did not wither away and become ill, as we would suppose to be the case if we were to consider without preconception the continuation of those impulses alone, which existed in humanity previous to the seventh and eighth centuries before Christ. Humanity does not wither away, does not become ill—on the contrary, it receives into itself a certain ingredient which has a healing influence from within. We see, here, the activity of a historical therapy.

Anyone who does not feel that the old Testament, and also the other ancient religions, point throughout to the fact that man's course of evolution is a gradual sickening process through sin—who does not see that humanity becomes ill through sin—cannot feel, on the other hand a certain something that radiates forth, and brings to the earth from outside, from outside the telluric sphere, a new influence in the same way that a new force enters the soil, when seeds are sown there. We learn to understand that a fructifying seed has been sown from supersensible worlds as a seed that brings healing; for humanity was indeed about to become ill. We learn to see, moreover, that something which is cosmic, and not merely telluric, enters the evolution of the earth, And when we learn to see in this way—when we see a Being entering historical evolution as the great invisible Therapeutist, we may then trace the personality of Jesus of Nazareth...it arises before us, even without the help or influence of the Gospels. For a search of this sort is not influenced by prejudice, but is led by a star—by something which is like the flashing forth of an inner light, which enables us to find the personality we have sought.

Thus, we really follow two different roads: on the one hand, we unite all sciences, including that one which takes into consideration in historical evolution, not merely the concepts "right" and "wrong", but also the concepts "healthy" and "ill". We adopt this synthetic science, and with it we approach the Mystery of Golgotha, just as the three Wise Men, or Magi from the East, approached it of old—with their ancient science and their starry lore. On the other hand, we may also approach this Mystery out of the simple feeling of the human heart—out of the true feelings of human nature.

If we meet the eternally-present Christ whom we can only find if we possess that organ into which the eternally present Christ says, in the spirit of St. Paul, "Not I, the Christ in me, makes me healthy, redeems me from death, giving me life again," we shall also find the man Jesus, in the history of humanity—the man Jesus, in whom the Christ actually lived.

In this way the super-terrestrial Being of the Christ, the Healer, the great Therapist, becomes united with the "simple man of Nazareth", who could not be otherwise than simple and gentle and who was able to speak to the poorest of the poor, who could also address his words to sinners, that is, to the diseased, but who spoke to them words which did not only contain what had been active within humanity up to that time—for in that case the words would have been as ill as those of the Roman period, because the words of the Romans were permeated merely by something abstract—who spoke to them words of everlasting life, which appealed not only to their understanding, but also to their feelings, to that which is irrational.

Thus we see that we can approach the personality of Jesus of Nazareth, and that we learn to know all the wonderful sides of his character described in the Gospel of St. Luke. But we are also led to all that the Gospel of St. John describes out of inner experience concerning the Healer, the Therapist, who is also the living Logos, the health-bringing Logos. We learn to connect the synoptic Gospels with the Gospel of St. John in the same moment when we no longer approach historical research with the rationalistic idea of what is formally right or wrong, but rather approach historical research with the higher ideas of healthy and ill. Thus the man Jesus loses nothing. For, inasmuch as He was chosen to take up within himself the healing impulse of the Christ, he does not require all the wisdom of ancient times, the development of which degenerated into a process of illness, so that humanity could no longer recognise the godly element through wisdom, but was only able to recognise, in a pathological way, the exterior natural aspect of things. We learn to know the One who, owing to the fact that He was fructified from above, became entirely that Being who wandered across the land of Palestine. We learn to consider the personality of Jesus as the outward sheath of the extra-terrestrial Being of the Christ. And we learn to realise that the earth would have lost its meaning, that it would have perished through illness, had the great healing-process through the Mystery of Golgotha not taken place.

Christianity does not lose the irrational, the paradoxical element. Man is only led in a right way toward that which no "ratio" can understand, toward that which can only be understood through a vitalised knowledge such as Anthroposophical research strives to bring to man. We see, on the contrary, that precisely the investigation of the life of Jesus has gradually become rationalistic, that the "simple man of Nazareth" has become the one and only reality for many people, and that they cannot find the Christ again. However, it is not possible to find the Christ through mere logic, even if it is historical logic. The Christ can only be found if we are able to trace the process of history with higher ideas—higher in this connection—such as healthy and ill. Then we indeed come to the point where we realise that the illnes that would gradually have befallen man, through the awakening of the Ego, would have led to the death of the spirit. For man would have gradually belonged more and more to Nature, owing to the extension of the Ego, arising out of the body. Nature would have spread over his soul. Man would gradually have fallen a prey to earthly death, and finally to the earth's death through heat.

If we realise that the impulse brought by the Mystery of Golgotha is one which gives a new meaning to the earth, we then find, precisely in historical evolution—through the Man, Jesus himself, through the death on the Cross and through resurrection—what the earth has received anew, from Heaven. We learn to know the meaning of the words, "this is my well beloved Son; this day, He is born unto me". We learn to know that, with this moment, a truly new Age begins to dawn upon the earth. We learn to know that human beings must gradually educate themselves, in order to understand what has entered human evolution through the Mystery of Golgotha. And we ask: In what way does this Mystery of Golgotha continue to influence mankind?

Now, my dear friends, at the time the Mystery of Golgotha took place on earth, there was still present something of what, in ancient times, had existed all over the earth, as a matter of fact—namely, a certain instinctive knowledge. Man possessed this knowledge, even though the development of the Ego had not as yet begun. The human being of ancient times did not possess a clearly-defined Ego; but, on the other hand, he had an instinctive knowledge which had been bestowed upon him through an instinctive divine inspiration. This constituted, in ancient times, the healthy element—this was the therapeutic original revelation. But this primordial revelation gradually vanished. The Ego began to extend itself over the whole human being; and, for this very reason, man became more and more ill. Nevertheless, there still existed a few last traces of an ancient, clairvoyant, instinctive knowledge concerning the spiritual worlds.

The Apostles still possessed such traces of an old clairvoyance. Also the Gnostics and many others possessed it—although, in the case of the Gnostics, these traces were not always perfect, or even adequate. Thus, it came about that the Christ could still be recognised with the aid of these inherited remnants of a true, ancient clairvoyance belonging to the past; people were still able to know that an extra-terrestrial Being had appeared in Jesus—a Being that had never before lived on the earth.

It was Paul who experienced this more profoundly than anyone. As Saul, he had already, to a certain extent, been intitiated in all the Mysteries in which it was possible to be initiated—out of the waning light of the ancient Wisdom. It was out of this waning light of the ancient Wisdom that he had opposed and combated the Christ-Jesus. In the very moment, however, that a supersensible vision arose in his inner being—the very moment the Christ appeared before him, as the Eternally-present

One—Paul turned toward the Cross on Golgotha. The inner experience of the Christ brought him to the outer experience of the Christ. Thus he was able to call himself an Apostle, to take his place among the Apostles—indeed, as the last of their number. Just as the Apostles and the Disciples were still able to exalt themselves to an experience of the Christ—through the forces which they had inherited from ancient clairvoyant times—in the same way that they were able to understand the resurrection, so also was Paul able to understand it. But, with the extension of the Ego, this understanding gradually vanished.

I might say that Theosophy has more and more become theology. Through logic, man gradually abandons his existence as a purely Nature-Being, and enters, in place of this, into the development of his Ego—which, at the same time, alternately leads him to that tendency to illness, of which we have already spoken.

The course of evolution—if it does not wish to lose the understanding of the Christ—must return again to the possibility of recognising the Christ as a supersensible, superterrestrial Being—in order that the personality of Jesus may be valued in the right way. Thus, we can also understand everything that has taken place since the time of the Apostles—of the Apostolic Fathers. We understand the struggles, the living struggles which took place throughout the centuries—influenced by the waning knowledge of the past and by the gradually-developing Ego-consciousness—those struggles to attain to a vision of the historical Christ.

It is not a new religion, or a new sect, that Anthroposophy wishes to found; but, if it simply pursues its own path and attains to supersensible knowledge, it must come face to face with the Mystery of Golgotha—not merely as one among many other events of earth, but as that event which gives the earth its particular meaning. Anthroposophy teaches us, moreover, that what mere "ratio" (reason) would cease to understand, can be understood again through supersensible vision. Anthroposophy can again—by following that path of knowledge which, as we have indicated, is not a rationalistic path—make known, the inner, Divine Being of Christ, in addition to the external, historical personality of Jesus. And the concept of Christ-Jesus thus acquires again the fullness of content—only that it is a concept which humanity must obtain through freedom.

This concept of Christ-Jesus may reveal itself, as it were, on the path followed by the poor shepherds—who at first divine inwardly the eternal Christ and then seek Him outwardly, in the Child, Jesus. But it is not only—as many would believe—along the path taken by the poor shepherds, that we can reach the Christ-Jesus; for, in that case, science would, in spite of everything, arise like a Moloch and swallow up so simple a faith. We can also—if we truly master science—find again that star which leads to Bethlehem. In the same way that the simplest human heart can find the Christ, through profound inner experience—if it rises, not merely to "ratio", but to a feeling of its own inner condition of illness—so this consciousness of being ill, which in its essence is none other than the feeling of a consciousness of sin, may lead, in a quite simple and natural way to the experience of the Christ, to a meeting with the Christ. On the other hand, *science* also cannot lead us away from this experience; for, if science attains—as in time it must attain, in all its spheres of learning—to a supersensible vision, then the highest form of science, as well as the simplest feelings of men's hearts, will find the Christ in the Man, Jesus. This is what Anthroposophy would strive, in a modest way, to achieve, It does not attempt to eliminate the mystery sought in reverent trustfulness by the simple human heart; for the path followed by Anthroposophy leads, it is true, to the higher spheres of knowledge, but it does not lead to rationalism...it must be careful to avoid, as I have already explained, the precipices of the irrational and the paradoxical. Indeed, it must substitute for "right" and "wrong" the life-filled concepts of "healthy" and "ill". To a mere physical therapy, it must add the great historical therapy.

Anthroposophical investigation—if it succeeds in rising to the knowledge to which it strives to rise—will then lead to the same truth which may at first reveal itself to a trusting reverence, as the true mystery, that which must remain concealed. Why do we speak of this unknown, hidden element?

Now, my dear friends, if we know a person, not merely through descriptions—if we do not simply believe in his existence, but are led before his countenance—we can then *see* him, we have a vision of the person. Yet, such a vision does not therefore have to be rationalistic. The irrational element in the person standing before us does not thereby cease to exist. He remains a mystery to us; for he possesses within him something that is intensively, profoundly infinite. No sort of "ratio" would be able to exhaust the wealth of his being.

In the same way, Anthroposophical knowledge cannot possibly exhaust the wealth of Christ—even though it may strive with the greatest longing, and with all the means of knowledge at its disposal, to reach the goal of *seeing* the Christ, not only of believing in Him. He does not cease to stand before us as a Being that cannot be grasped by "ratio" alone, even when we are able to see Him. And, in the same way that a human being does not necessarily lose any of the reverence which we may feel for him, as we feel it for every human being, just because he remains a mystery, even when we are led before his countenance—so the Mystery of Golgotha remains a Mystery, and is not drawn down by Anthroposophy into dry abstractions and logical rationalism. Anthroposophy does not in the least strive to eliminate the "irrational" and the "paradoxical", in Christianity, through the Christ-Jesus it reveals to us; it strives rather, to *see* this irrational and paradoxical element. What we are able to see may fill us with just as great a measure of deep and childlike reverence as what we are merely expected to believe—perhaps, indeed, with an even deeper and an even more childlike reverence.

For this reason, Anthroposophy does not kill faith, but fills it with life. This may be seen, especially in the way in which it seeks to unravel the Mystery of Golgotha—the union of the Christ, with the personality of Jesus.

At the same time, all of this, my dear friends, is of course, the object of an extensive research, carried on over a number of years—indeed, a research which has only just begun. And I must ask your pardon, if I have pointed out only a few fundamental truths in this lecture—which has already been far too long. Yet, perhaps these fundamental lines or thoughts may at least make clear to you that Anthroposophy does not in the least strive to draw us down into the rationalism of ordinary knowledge; nor does it wish to make of the Mystery of Golgotha a mystery that has been irreverently unveiled. It seeks, rather, to lead us to the Mystery of Golgotha. with the greatest possible reverence, with the deepest religious feelings—indeed, with a deepened religious feeling, which becomes more profound when, for the first time, we are seized with a feeling of true awe in the presence of the Cross on Golgotha.

Thus Anthroposophy does not wish to contribute toward a deadening of Christianity, but seeks, on the contrary, to fill it with new life—with a new soul-content; for it appears, to be suffering painfully under the influence of rationalism, which is fully justified only in the sphere of external natural science.

THE NECESSITY FOR A RENEWAL OF CULTURE

I have been asked to lecture this evening on The Necessity for a Renewal of Culture. During the past few days I have been speaking to you on the spiritual science of Anthroposophy. This is a field which may be dealt with generally by any individual, if he thinks that he can communicate to others this or that result of special investigations or impulses. For this is the expression of an individual impulse—although one must of course bear in mind that it is something which, from certain standpoints, may be of interest to all.

But I have quite a different feeling in regard to this evening's subject. In the present time, when one has to speak of the necessity for a renewal of culture, one only has the right to do so if one can perceive that this subject really corresponds to a general demand, that people are filled by the desire for a renewal of culture, and believe in what may be called a renewal of culture. An individual must therefore more or less interpret a generally ruling view. For, in regard to such a subject arbitrary individual opinions would only be an expression of lack of modesty and conceit.

*Translated from stenographic notes unrevised by the lecturer.

The following question therefore arises : Does this subject correspond to-day to a generally ruling feeling, to a sum of feelings which exists in wide circles ? If we look in an unprejudiced way into the hearts and souls of our contemporaries, if we study their soul-moods and their general frame of mind, we may indeed believe that this subject of the necessity for a renewal of culture is in many respects justified.

Do we not see that in the most varied spheres of life many of our contemporaries feel that something must penetrate into our spiritual life and into the other branches of human life, something which in some way corresponds to the longing which manifests itself so clearly ?

To-day we come across searching souls in many fields of artistic life. Who has not noticed these searching souls ? We find them above all among modern youth. Particularly there we find that youth expects something which it cannot obtain from the things offered by the generally prevailing spirit of the times. Especially in the sphere of ethical-religious life we come across such seeking souls. Innumerable questions, expressed and above all unexpressed, questions which live only in the depths of feeling, are now reposing in human hearts. If we consider social life, then the course of the world's events and all that takes place, as it were, within this domain, takes on the aspect of *one* great question : Where must we look for some kind of cultural renewal of our social life ?

The individual, however, who considers these different questions, may nevertheless not go further than the belief that he can but offer a small contribution towards these problems, arising out of a generally felt need in this domain. But perhaps the explanations resulting from anthroposophical spiritual research contained in the last lectures which I gave to you here, entitle me to set forth a few facts on the subject chosen for to-day, even though the spiritual science of Anthroposophy knows that in regard to many things which people are now seeking, it can at the most offer a few impulses which can bear fruit; yet it is the very aim of anthroposophical research to offer such impulses, such germinating forces.

At Dornach, in Switzerland, we have tried to establish the School for Spiritual Science, the Goetheanum. Here we can say that at least the attempt has been made to fructify the single scientific spheres by adding to the results obtained in medicine, natural science, sociology, history, and many other fields by the highly significant methods of recent times, the results which can be obtained through direct investigation of the spiritual world itself.

In the pedagogical-didactical field, the effort has been made to obtain some practical results through the Waldorf School in Stuttgart. Attempts have even been made to achieve results in the economic field. But there we must say that present conditions are so difficult, that these newly founded economic undertakings must first pass the test showing whether they are able to—I will not say attain—but at least encourage what so many modern people are seeking to find.

Let me therefore begin with this quest. I cannot speak of course from the standpoint of your nation, where I have the great pleasure of being your guest; I can only speak to you from an international standpoint. Those who have open hearts, minds and souls for the longings of that section of mankind which counts most for the future, those who observe this in an unprejudiced way, cannot help turning their gaze to the young people and their quest!

Everywhere we find that our young people are filled with the longing, arising out of an altogether indefinite feeling, for something quite new. The earnest, significant question must therefore rise up: Why do our young people not find full satisfaction in the things which we as older people could offer to them? And I believe that this very quest of youth is connected with the most intimate and deepest soul-impulses, which give rise in men's hearts in the present time to this general sense of seeking.

I believe that in this respect we must penetrate deeply into human souls, if the call for a renewal of culture, which can now be heard plainly, is to be judged according to its true foundation. We shall have to look into many depths of human soul-life; above all we cannot deal only with the characteristics of modern culture, but we shall have to survey a longer stretch of time.

If we do this in an unprejudiced way, we find that in an international respect the special soul-configuration of modern humanity has been prepared during the past three, four or five centuries, and we also find that these last three, four and five centuries reveal something completely new, compared with the spiritual constitution which still existed in the Occident during the 10th, 11th and 12th centuries, derived from a still earlier epoch. Whenever we survey these earlier times of spiritual life in the Occident, we find that man's soul-spiritual conception was not so strictly separated from his physical or sensory conception, as was the case later on and during the present time.

In earlier centuries, when the human being turned his senses towards the physical world which constituted his environment, he always knew that a spiritual element also lived in the objects which he perceived though his senses. He no longer had such a highly spiritual conception of the world as, for instance, the ancient Egyptian, or even the ancient Greek, who saw the external embodiment of soul-spiritual beings in the world of the stars, but he still had some inkling of the fact that a spiritual essence permeated everything in his physical environment.

Again, when the human being of earlier centuries looked back upon his own self, he did not strictly separate his physical-bodily part from his soul, i.e. from thought, feeling and will. I might say that by being conscious of his soul, he was at the same time conscious of the members of his body, of the organs of his body, and he also perceived a soul-spiritual essence in these bodily organs, he felt a soul-spiritual essence in his own organism. In the world outside he experienced this soul-spiritual essence, and within his own self he also experienced a soul-spiritual essence.

He thus felt a certain relationship, a certain intimacy with the world around him. He could say to himself: What lives within me, also lives in a certain respect within the universe, and Divine-spiritual beings, who lead and guide the world, placed me into this universe. He felt connected with the universe and had a feeling of intimacy with it. He experienced, as it were, that he formed part of the great soul-spiritual-physical organism of the universe.

This is a feeling which we do not fully understand to-day, because during the past centuries the times have undergone a complete change. This change appears not only among theoreticians and scientists, but it reveals itself in every human heart, in every human soul. It does not merely reveal itself in the way in which modern people contemplate the world, but also in the way in which spirit is embodied in matter in artistic creation and in the enjoyment of art. It reveals itself in our social life, in the way in which we face our fellowman, in the understanding which we have for him, and in what we demand from him. Finally it reveals itself in the feelings which we have concerning our own ethical - religious impulses, in the way in which we experience the Divine within our own heart and soul, in our attitude towards the impulse which gave to the earth in the deepest way the key to the spirit underlying earthly existence — in our attitude towards the deeper inner meaning of Christianity.

We can therefore say: What people thus search for in widest circles must in some way be related with this change. What is the nature of this change?

Now the last centuries have seen the dawn of an age which is frequently described as the age of intellectualism. But it was not intellectualism, an abstract use of the understanding which in the past made people feel so closely connected and acquainted with the surrounding world—as I briefly explained to you just now. Only in the course of human evolution has modern man thoroughly learned to have full confidence in the intellect and in the understanding, when contemplating the world, and even when experiencing it.

Now, however, there are two conditions of human life which are interrelated: inwardly, intellectualism and confidence in the authority of reason, of the understanding, and outwardly, faith in the phenomena of Nature and a sense for the observation of Nature's phenomena.

Inwardly, modern man developed an inclination to set everything under the rule of an intellectualistic observation based on reason. As a natural consequence, this inner capacity above all, could only be applied to the phenomena of Nature, to everything which can be observed through the senses, to everything which can be analysed or combined in the form of thoughts. These two things, I might say, the indisputable observation of Nature and the development of the intellect, were the two great, important means of education used during recent centuries: they exercised their strongest influence upon civilised humanity during the 19th century and have also carried their fruits into the 20th century.

One of the characteristics connected with the use of the intellect is that in a certain way our inner experience becomes isolated. The use of the intellect (it clearly reveals itself in its picture-character) in a certain way estranges feeling; it takes on a cold, prosaic life-nuance, and in reality it can only develop in the right way through external Nature, through everything which constitutes the surrounding world.

Through this connection, through this relationship of man with the world, deeply satisfying explanations can be found in regard to Nature, but it does not supply in the same measure as in the past the possibility to discover oneself, as it were, within external Nature. The soul-spiritual element which shone out to the men of olden times from a world filled with colour, sound, warmth and coldness, and from the year's seasons, could be experienced as something which was related to what lived in their inner being.

Through our feeling, we can no longer directly bring into our own inner being the whole external life of Nature, which we learn to know through the intellect—all that we discover through intellectual research in physics, chemistry and biology. We can certainly strive to investigate biologically man's inner organic structure; we can even go as far as seeking to investigate the chemical processes of the human organism. But if we apply the investigation of external Nature to the human organism in order to understand it, we shall never find that this manner of investigation also takes hold of our feeling, that it can be summed up in a religious-ethical feeling towards the universe, and that finally it can be expressed in the feeling: " I am a member of the universe: Soul-spiritual is the universe, and I too am soul-spiritual."

This feeling does not shine out of the things which could be learnt during recent centuries through the magnificent impulses of natural science. Consequently, the very forces which brought the best and most significant fruit and which transformed the whole existence of modern man, at the same time estranged him from his own self.

The fact that he stands within the universe and admiringly looks upon his mathematical conception of the spatial world, of the stars and their movements, the fact that he can unfathom with a certain scientific reverence what plants, animals, etc., contain, is accompanied (in spite of all the problems which are still unsolved) by a certain feeling of satisfaction; people are filled with satisfaction that on the one hand it is possible for them to solve the riddles of Nature by using their intellect and their reason; but there is one thing which cannot be reached along this path, namely a *Knowledge of Man's True Being*.

The science dealing with the stars, the science which exists in the form of physics and chemistry, the science of biology, and in more recent times even the science of history, do not reveal anything in reply to man's deepest longing concerning his own being. And hence arose more and more the need to seek for something else.

Their quest is none other than the *quest of modern man for the human being*. Though we may do our utmost to summarise the true nature of this quest in different spheres everywhere, we find that men now really wish to solve the riddle of their own being, the riddle of man.

This is not merely something which may interest theoreticians, but something which deeply penetrates into the constitution of every human soul. To all who are interested in such things it is undoubtedly a source of deepest longing when the investigation of Nature leads to the desire to discover also what lies concealed behind the great expanse of Nature's life : namely, man's being, which greatly transcends all that can be gathered from the external kingdoms of Nature.

But I might say : At this point, the great riddle, the search for the nature of man, really begins. At this point we also understand the fact that we have allowed our feelings and our whole education to be influenced by forces which thus came to the fore during recent centuries. External life reflects this in every way. Far more than we think, external life reflects the forces which came to the fore in the spiritual life of humanity during its more recent course of development, as described just now.

We not only enquire in vain after man's true being from a theoretical standpoint,—oh no !— but to-day we pass each other by, and under the influence of our modern education we have not the capacity to understand our fellow-men inwardly, we lack the capacity to look with a kind of clairvoyant sympathy into the human soul and into what lives in it, a capacity which still existed in many civilisations of the past. Not only theoretically have we lost the understanding for the human being, but in every moment of the day we lack a sympathetic comprehension, a sympathetic, feeling contact with our fellow-men. Perhaps this appears most clearly of all in the social question; in its present form it shows us that we have indeed lost this understanding for our fellow-men.

For why does the call for social reforms, for a social renewal, resound so loudly? Because in reality we have grown utterly unsocial. As a rule we demand most loudly of all the very things which we most sorely lack, and in the loud call for socialism, a truly unprejudiced person can hear the truth, that we no longer understand each other and are unable to build up a social organism, because we have grown so unsocial. Consequently, we cling to the hope that our understanding, which has reached such a high stage of development through intellectualism, may after all lead us back to an organic social structure.

The social question itself shows us above all how estranged we have become from each other as human beings. In quite recent times the religious question confronts us, because we have lost the immediate inner experience of being directly connected with the divine essence of the universe; we no longer feel the voice speaking within our own self as an expression of the Divine-spiritual. The call for a religious renewal also arises through a really felt need.

If we now look more deeply into the seeking life of modern times, by setting out from such aspects, we find that the intellectual culture, the intellectual contemplation which gradually made even human feeling grow pale, is after all something which is connected with a definite age of human life.

We should not fall a prey to any illusion: for in regard to his intellect, the human being really awakes only when he reaches the age of puberty; his intellectual powers awake at that time of his life when he is ready to work in the external world. But intellectualism is never our own personal property, a force which can move our soul during childhood, or soon after when we go to school. In this early life the soul's configuration must differ from its later configuration. The intellectual element in modern life cannot and *must not* develop during childhood and in early youth, for it would have a chilling, deadening, paralyzing effect upon the forces of youth.

Thus it came about (in order to understand the present time and its longings we must penetrate into more intimate details of life) that we now grow into a culture which deprives us—though this may sound paradoxical—in our mature age of the most beautiful memories of our childhood.

If we look back in memory upon our experiences of childhood, we cannot draw up with sufficient intensity and warmth the undefined feelings and memories which frequently live in unconscious depths and which sometimes can only rise up in nuances of thoughts and memories. We reach the point of being unable to understand ourselves completely. We look back upon the life of our childhood as if it were a riddle. We no longer know how to speak out of our full human being, and into the language which we speak as grown-ups we can no longer bring that shading which re-echoes what the child experiences in its living wisdom, when it turns its innocent eyes to the surrounding world, when it unfolds its will during the early years of its existence.

We do not study history in a true way if it does not show us that among the people of olden times, the speech of men who had reached a mature age always re-echoed the development of childhood. We live through our childhood unconsciously, but in such a way, that this unconscious life of the soul still contains in an intensive form what we brought with us through birth, through the union with the physical body, what we brought with us from the soul-spiritual life of our pre-existence.

Those who can observe a child, those who have an open soul and mind for this kind of observation, will discover the greatest mystery when they see how week by week the child unfolds what the human being brings with him into the earthly-physical world from a soul-spiritual existence. What man's eternal being unconsciously brings into the human members, into the whole human organisation, so that it lives and pulses through the body, brings about an inner permeation with soul-spiritual forces, which however encounter a kind of chilling substance, when later on the intellect which really exists only for earthly concerns comes to the fore.

Those who to-day have enough self-observation for such intimate things, know that a kind of thin fog spreads over that which seeks to enter our mature consciousness from our childhood; they know that it is impossible to bring into words which have grown old the living experiences of childhood, because these exercise a soul-spiritual influence, and live within the child in a far more intensive soul-spiritual form than they can later on live in an intellectualistic state.

A witty writer of the 18th and 19th century once wrote : During his first three years of life, man learns far more than during his three years at the university. I do not mean to hurt the feelings of university students, for I can appreciate them, but I also believe that in regard to our whole, full manhood, we learn more during the first three years of life, when we form our organism out of our still unconscious wisdom, than we can ever learn later on. Yet our modern culture strongly develops the tendency to forget these most important three years of life, at least it has the tendency to prevent their coming to expression in a corresponding living way in that which manifests itself later on as the expression of our mature culture. But this fact exercises a great influence upon our whole civilised life. If we are unable to colour, animate, and spiritualise our mature speech and the thoughts of mature life with the forces which well up from our own childhood,—because the intellect gives us pictures, a spiritual world in pictures, but is unable to absorb spiritual life, the life of the spirit itself—if we are unable to do this, we cannot speak to youth in a living and intensive way. We then speak out of a lost youth to a living youth round about us.

This is the feeling which we discover in modern youth, this is the feeling expressed in their search and which may be characterised as follows: " You old people speak a language which we cannot understand; you speak words which find no echo in our hearts and souls."—This is why the call for a renewal of culture is to be heard above all in the longings of our young people, and we must realise that by going back to a comprehension of the spiritual we must again learn to speak to youth in the right way, and even to speak in the right way to children.

My dear friends, those who permeate their inner being with the truths which anthroposophical spiritual research seeks to grasp through the soul's living being and not through abstract thoughts, take hold of something which does not grow old, which even in mature years does not deprive them of the forces of childhood; they feel, in a certain way, the more spiritual forces of childhood and of youth entering their maturer life. They will then find the words and the deeds which appeal to youth, the words and deeds which unite them with the young.

It was this observation of youth's mood of seeking which led to the endeavour to create at the Waldorf School in Stuttgart above all a body of teachers able to speak to children out of a spiritual rejuvenation reached in maturer years, to speak to children once more as if they were real friends. To those people who acquire something of genuine spirituality in their life, every child is a revelation, they know that the child, the small child and the older child, can—if they have an open heart for this—give them more than they can give to the child. Though this may sound paradoxical, it is nevertheless the note which may lead to a kind of renewal of culture in this sphere.

If we let this shed light on the other things which confront us in life, we must say to ourselves: If we clearly perceive that man is in search of man and that he must seek him; that is to say, if we can see that the human being who has become one-sided through intellectualism goes in search of the full whole human being, we shall come across this same fact very definitely in many other spheres of life to-day.

If we survey the times which have given rise to the great achievements of modern culture, achievements which cannot be prized highly enough, we find that modern civilisation could only be gained by forfeiting something of man's whole being. Man looked out into the world's spaces. He could build instruments enabling him to discover the nature and the movements of the stars. It is only since a few centuries, however, that results which thus confront us have developed in such a way as to supply a mathematical physical picture of the universe. To-day we no longer feel how in the past men looked out into the universe and perceived in the stars' courses a revelation of the spirit in the cosmos, in the same way in which we now perceive in the physiognomy of a human being the revelation of his soul and spirit. An abstract, dried-up mathematical-mechanical element now appears to us in the cosmos, although in itself it is one which cannot be prized highly enough. We look up to the sky and perceive nothing but an immense world-mechanism. The ideal has more and more gained ground to perceive this world--mechanism everywhere. And what has grown out of it to-day?

Though to many contemporaries this may still seem contradictory, I think that to an unprejudiced observation it is everywhere clearly evident that the social sphere of humanity which surrounds us everywhere and which constitutes our modern civilisation, now sends out its answers to the concept of world-mechanism.

For to-day our social and also our ethical and juridical life, and in a certain way—as I will immediately show you—even our religious life, have taken on a mechanistic character.

We can see that in millions and millions of men there lives the view that the historical evolution of mankind does not contain spiritual forces, but only economic forces, and that everything which lives in art, religion, ethics, science, law, etc., is a kind of fog rising out of the only historical reality, out of economic life. Economic forms are realities and their influence upon men—this is what many people say to-day and one's heart should feel the great tragedy of such statements— gives rise to what develops in the form of law, ethics, religion, art, etc. This is their view: they think that all this is an ideology.

This has driven us in a direction which has, to be sure, produced great results in the spiritual life of the Occident, but to-day it has reached the opposite pole of what once existed in ancient better times of the past in the civilisation of the Orient—though even the Oriental culture has now become decadent. It was a one-sided culture, but our modern culture is also one-sided.

Let us bear in mind that once upon a time—in the East above all—there lived a race which described the external physical world as Maya, as the great illusion, for it only looked upon man's inner life as the true reality, man's thoughts, sensations, feelings and impulses of the will were the only reality. Once upon a time there was this other one-sided conception of perceiving the true essence and reality only in man's inner being, in the world of his thoughts, feelings and sensations, and of seeing in the external world nothing but Maya or the great illusion.

To-day we have reached the opposite conception, which is also one-sided. From the standpoint of modern culture we see the physical world everywhere round about us, and we call it the true reality. Millions of people see reality only in the physical course of economic processes and consider man's inner life an ideology, with the inclusion of everything which has proceeded from it in the development of culture. What millions and millions of people now designate an ideology is after all the same thing which the Orientals once called Maya, illusion,—it is simply a different word, and used to be sure, in the opposite sense. The Oriental could have applied the word " ideology " to the external world, and " reality " to his inner being. Modern culture has reached the stage that countless people now apply these words in an opposite one-sidedness.

Our social life reveals something of which we can say: It has resulted in great and significant triumphs for science, but it has brought difficulties into human life itself, into the ethical and social life of men. But this mechanisation of life which now faces us does not only live in the ideas of millions of men, it really also exists. Our external life has become mechanised, and with our modern culture we are now living in a time which supplies man's answer in the social, ethical and religious spheres of life.

What first arose as a conception of the world in the great age of Galileo, Copernicus and Giordano Bruno, the conception which was then born, demands to be sure that it should be permeated with humanity in a different way from what has been the case so far. For the mechanisation of our human life is, as it were, the answer of civilisation to the mechanical character of our intellectual, scientific life.

We can see this in every detail. To-day we study natural science. We study the development of animal species from the lowest, simplest, most imperfect forms right up to man. Guided by highly praiseworthy scientific thought, we then place man at the end of this line of organic beings. What does this teach us in regard to him? That he is the highest animal. This is, of course, significant in a certain way, but we thus only learn to know man in his relationship to the other beings, not as he experiences himself as man. We learn to know what man develops in regard to the other beings, but not what constitutes his own self. *Man loses himself* in as much as he contemplates the external world in accordance with the admirable principles of modern natural science.

And hence the search for the human being, since through the great achievements of modern time, man has in a certain way, lost himself. And if we then look at the communal life in the social organism, we find that their reciprocal actions compel men to live as they do. In regard to this necessity we have gone very far in modern times. Into every sphere of social life there has entered a division of work. As regards the external mechanised life of modern times we must work so as to realise the truth of the words: All for one and one for all! In regard to external life we have had to learn to work one for the other.

But also here we can see that for those who have not preserved old traditions but who have grown into the most modern form of life, human labour has become completely separated from the human being and that our modern understanding only enables us to grasp the external nature of man. Our conception and feeling in regard to human labour, through which we help our fellow men and work together with them, has therefore become a purely external one. We no longer observe the man and how he develops his work out of his soul-spiritual existence on earth, we do not see how human labour is the outcome of a man with whom we are closely bound up through feeling, who is a being like us. We see him and we do not feel that he is working for us. No, in the social life of to-day we look at the product, we see how much human labour has flowed into it and we judge human work in so far as we find it in the product.

This is so deeply rooted in people's minds, that by enhancing this great error of modern times Karl Marx reached the point of designating everything circulating as human labour in the form of goods produced for human consumption, as a crystallised condensed labour. We now judge labour separated from the human being, in the same way in which we have acquired the power of observing Nature apart from man. Our judgement of human labour is really infected by what we have learned to know concerning man and by the way in which we look upon him through natural science. This only leads us as far as the Nature-side of man, only as far as the fact that man is the highest animal : we do not penetrate as far as man's innermost being.

Even when we observe man in his work, we do not see how this work comes from him, but we wait instead until the product is there and only seek the work in something which has become emancipated from the man. And there stands man among us as a social being who knows that he must put into labour his human nature and frequently his human dignity, and he sees that this human dignity and the way in which labour comes out of his inner self, is not valued ; human work is only valued when it has streamed into the external product which is then brought on to the market ; labour is there something which has been submerged in the wares, something which can, as it were, be bought and sold.

So in this connection too we see how man has lost himself. He has forfeited, as it were, a piece of his own self—his work—to the mechanism of modern civilisation.

We see this above all in the juridical part of the social organism. If we observe how the spiritual, mental, life prevails among us in modern times we find that the spirit only exists in abstract thoughts; that we can only have confidence in abstract thoughts and forget that the spirit lives within us in a direct way, that the spirit enters into us whenever we occupy ourselves with it, that our soul is not only filled by thoughts, but that our soul is really penetrated by the spirit whenever we are spiritually active. Mankind has lost this connection with the spirit, while its conception of Nature has become great. This in regard to the spiritual life.

In regard to our juridical, social and political life, the example of human labour has shown us that something which is connected with the human being has been torn away from him. When we observe the human soul in its intercourse as man with man, we do not see feeling flashing up and growing warm when one person looks at another's work. There is no warm feeling for the man at his work. We do not see the work developing in connection with man, but we only see something which can no longer kindle the other man's warm sympathy; we see the labour after it has left the man, and has flowed into the product.

So in this sphere too, in the sphere of human intercourse and juridical life, we have lost man.

And if we look at the sphere of economics: in the economic life man must procure for himself what he needs for his consumption. The things which he needs for his own consumption are those for which he develops his capacities. Man will work all the better for others, for himself and for the whole human community, the more he develops his capacities. The essential point in economic life is the development of human faculties. When it is a question of people, an employee will find it advantageous to work for a capable employer. This is quite possible, for those whose work is guided by others physically or spiritually, soon recognise that they fare better with a capable leader than with an incapable one.

But does our modern economic striving tend above all to bear in mind the economic life and activity of mankind and to ask everywhere : Where are the more capable people ? If we were to look upon this living element in man, upon this purely human element, if people were placed into economic life in accordance with their capacities, so that they might achieve their best for their fellows: that could achieve a conception, a culture, able to discover the human being in man.

But the characteristic of our modern culture is just this, that it cannot discover the human being in man, and to an unprejudiced observation it is evident that we have gradually lost the power of judging people rightly, in accordance with their capacities and gifts.

To be sure that testing entity, the examination, through which men's capacities are supposed to be shown, has acquired a great importance in our modern civilisation. But its chief aim is not to discover how a person can most capably work in life, for the mechanised way of living requires something else. In many respects indeed, there is the call to-day to let the best man fill the best place according to requirement, but this generally remains a pious wish, and we see that economic life above all—as well as other spheres, such as spiritual and juridical life—becomes severed from the human being. We do not consider the human being above all and his living connection with economic life, but we consider instead the best way in which he can become connected with something which is not really related to man. We see that economic life as well is separating itself from man. It is therefore no wonder that the call for a renewal of our present culture should arise in every sphere of life under the aspect of a search for the human being.

Things are not much better in the sphere of *art*. If we look back into the times of ancient Greece, we think that the Greek tragedians wrote their dramas in the same way in which we write them now. Yet the Greek conception of life in no way resembles the present one. The Greek spoke of Catharsis, the purification which must take place through the drama. What did he understand by catharsis or purification ?—He meant that a person participating in the action of such a tragedy or of some other piece, experienced something in his soul which made him pass through certain feigned emotions. But this had a purifying effect, and thereby a healing effect upon him, reaching as far as the physical organism; it had above all a purifying and healing effect upon the soul. And the most important thing in Greek drama consisted both in a higher spiritual impulse and, I might say, in a medical impulse; the Greek saw a kind of healing process in what he wished to impart to his fellow-men through his highly perfected art.

We cannot of course, become Greeks again; I am merely telling you this as an elucidation of the fact that we have actually entered into a mechanised way of living which is, as it were, a denial of the human being, and that this explains the deep longing which passes through the modern world as a search for man.

The spiritual science of Anthroposophy in order to support this search for the human being, strives for what may be called the *threefold division of the social organism.* This is subjected to many misunderstandings. It only seeks ways, however, which will lead, in the life of the spirit, to the rediscovery of no mere abstract spirit, a pallid thought world, at most a reflecting upon the spirit; which will lead, in the juridical-political life, to the rediscovery of not merely the work that flows into the product, but the valuing of man's work, that human valuing of work which arises in the communal life when man as man confronts his fellows in pure humanity.

And in the economic sphere, the threefold division of the social organism aims at the forming of Associations in which people unite as consumers and producers, so that they can guide economic life in an associative way, out of the most varied human spheres of interest.

We judge economic requirements purely through the mechanism of the market. The

Associations are meant to unite people as living human beings who recognise the requirements in economic life; they are to form an organism that can regulate the conditions of production determined by the common life of men and by a knowledge of these requirements arising from such a joint life.

The threefold division of the social organism thus seeks to connect these three members—spiritual life, juridical life and economic life—in such a way within the social organism that the human element may everywhere be found again in the free life of the spirit, that does not serve economic interests nor proceed from these, that does not serve political interests nor proceed from these, but that stands freely upon its own foundation and seeks to develop human capacities in the best way. This free life of the spirit seeks to show man the human being,—it shows the human being to man.

In the free Life of the Spirit the human being can be found by experiencing the spirit, thus unfolding in a harmonious way the human capacities; from such a relatively independent spiritual life, it will then be possible to send into the political-juridical life and into the economic life the men with the best capacities, thus fructifying these spheres. If the economic life or political life dictate what capacities are to be developed, they themselves cannot prosper. But if they leave the life of the spirit completely free, so that it can give to the world out of its own foundations what every individual brings into existence out of divine-spiritual worlds, then the other spheres of life can become fruitful in the widest sense of the word.

The States-life should cultivate what men can develop as the feeling of legal rights, as moral disposition inasmuch as they face each other as equals. The Economic Life should discover man through the necessary Associations in keeping with his needs and capacities in the economic sphere. The threefold division of the social organism does not aim at a mechanical separation of these three spheres, but by establishing a relative independence of these three spheres it seeks to enable man once more to find through these three spheres of life the full humanity which he has lost and which he is seeking to discover again.

In such a sense we may indeed speak of the necessity for a renewal of culture. And this is particularly evident if we look still deeper into man's inner being, into that inner part where, if he seeks to be fully man, and experience fully his dignity and worth as a human being, he must connect himself with the divine-spiritual; where he must experience and feel his own eternal being, that is to say, when we look at men's common religious life.

My dear friends, I only desire of course to say that these are the convictions of anthroposophical spiritual science; I do not wish to press anyone to accept this particular solution of to-day's subject. Anthroposophy seeks above all to recognise once more the place of Christianity in the evolution of the earth. It points to the Mystery of Golgotha, as Anthroposophy can unravel it in the spiritual world. Historical evolution is then traced in relation to the Mystery of Golgotha.

A spiritual study of human *history* reveals that in primeval times humanity possessed a kind of primeval revelation, a kind of instinctive primeval wisdom, which gradually disappeared and grew fainter, and this would have increased as time went on. If nothing else had occurred, we should now be living within a pallid spiritual life deprived of wisdom, a spiritual life that could have nothing in common with the warmth of our soul-life had not earthly existence been fructified at a certain moment by something which came from outside the earth.

Spiritual science, in the sense of Anthroposophy, can once more draw attention to the man Jesus, who at the beginning of our era, wandered upon the earth in Palestine. We see that modern external Christianity more and more considers this man Jesus merely as a human being, whereas in older times people saw in Jesus a Being from spiritual worlds transcending the earth, Who had united Himself with the man Jesus and Who had become Christ Jesus.

By investigating the spheres outside the earth with the aid of spiritual observation, spiritual science does not only draw attention to the man Jesus, but also to the Christ Who descended from heavenly heights, as a Principle transcending the earth and penetrating through the Mystery of Golgotha into human life on earth. And since the Mystery of Golgotha, the evolution of humanity on earth has become different, for a fructifying process from the heavenly worlds took place.

Modern culture leads men to concentrate their attention more and more upon the man Jesus, thus losing that feeling of genuine religious devotion gained by looking upon Christ Jesus, a feeling which alone can give us satisfaction. By looking only upon the man Jesus, people really lose that part in Jesus which could be of special value to them. For the human being in man has been lost. Even through religion we do not know how to seek in the right way the man in Jesus of Nazareth.

Through a deepening of the spiritual-religious life, anthroposophical spiritual science once more discloses the source of religious devotion, in other words, it leads to the search of the divine in man within the human being himself, so that it can also rediscover in the man Jesus the super-earthly Christ, thus penetrating to the real essence of Christ Jesus. Anthroposophy does not in any way degrade the Mystery of Golgotha by saying that what formerly existed outside the earth afterwards came down to the earth.

And what does one experience in the present age of modern culture by pursuing such a goal?

The tendency of anthroposophical spiritual science to consider what transcends the earthly sphere has led people to retort that Anthroposophy is not Christian, that it cannot be Christianity because it sets a super-earthly, cosmic Being in Christ Jesus in place of the purely human being. They even think that it is an offence to say that Christ came down from cosmic spaces and penetrated into Jesus. Why do they think this? Because people only see the mathematical-mechanical cosmos, only the great machinery, as it were, when they look out into the heavenly spaces, and this attitude affects even religion, even man's religious feeling. Consequently even religious people, and those who teach religion to-day, think that religion would be mechanised if Christ were to be sought in the cosmic spaces before the time of the Mystery of Golgotha. Yet spiritual science does not mechanise religion, nor does it deprive Christianity of its Christian element; instead it fills external life with Christianity by showing : out there in the cosmos is not mere mechanism, not merely phenomena and laws which can be grasped through mathematics and natural science,—there is spirituality.

Whereas modern theologians often believe that Anthroposophy speaks of a Christ coming down from the sun, from the lifeless cosmic space into Jesus, what is true is that Anthroposophy also sees the spiritual in the realms outside the earth, and considers it a blessing for the earth that the heavenly powers sent down their influence through this Being Who gave the earth its meaning by passing through the Mystery of Golgotha, by coming down from heavenly heights and uniting Himself with the evolution of humanity upon the earth.

The spiritual science of Anthroposophy thus really seeks to render religious life fruitful again and to fill it with real warmth; it seeks to lead man back to the original source of the divine. And this is sought by listening to what lies in the call for a renewal of our culture.

We have watched the development of a magnificent science and are full of admiration for the achievements of this modern science which have brought about such great results in our civilisation. But in addition to this, we realise that there exists the call for a renewal of religious life, for a renewed religious deepening. On the one hand, we are to have a science which has nothing to do with religion, and at the same time we are to have a religious renewal. This is the dream of many people.

But it will be a vain dream. For the content of religion can never be drawn out of anything but what a definite epoch holds to be knowledge. If we look back into times when religious life was fully active, we find that religions were also filled with the content of knowledge of a definite epoch, though in a special form, with the breath of reverence and piety, with true devotion and (this is specially significant) with a feeling of veneration for the founder of the particular religion.

Our present time, our modern civilisation, will therefore be unable to draw any satisfaction out of a religious content which does not harmonise with the knowledge which is accessible to modern people. That is why anthroposophical spiritual science does not seek a religion in addition to science, but it endeavours instead to raise science itself to a stage where it can once more become religious. It does not seek an irreligious science, and beside it an unscientific religion, but a science which can cultivate a religious life out of its own sources. For the science which Anthroposophy seeks is not based in a one-sided way upon the intellect, but it embraces the whole human being and everything which lives in him. Such a form of science does not have a destructive influence upon religious life, and above all it has no destructive influence upon Christian life, but will shed light upon it, so that one can find in the Mystery of Golgotha which entered the evolution of the earth the eternal, supersensible significance which was bestowed upon humanity through this event. If we look upon the Mystery of Golgotha, religious enthusiasm and inner religious happiness will enter our feelings and in a moral way also our will, and this religious life cannot be destroyed, but can be illumined in the right way by the truths which we can see and comprehend in regard to Christ Jesus, and His entrance into the earthly development of humanity.

Spiritual science therefore tries to meet the search for the human being. As I already explained to you, this lecture is only meant to be a small contribution to the hoped-for and longed-for renewal of our modern culture. It only seeks to explain the way in which it is possible to view the significance, the deep, inner, human significance of the longings which can find expression in a problem such as the renewal of modern culture.

In my lecture I also wished to show you that this call for a renewal of culture is really at the same time a call for knowledge for the development of a new feeling of the true human nature. The problem dealing with the nature of this search which strives after a renewal of modern culture is one which really exists, and we must seek to gain a real feeling of the true being of man, a full experience of the human being. Perhaps it is justified to believe that we may interpret this call for a renewal of culture, a call which is in many ways not at all clear and distinct, by saying to ourselves : The striving human being is now confronted in a really significant way by the renewal of a problem which resounded in ancient Greece and which now re-echoes from there in the call: " O man, know thyself ! "

Assuredly the noblest endeavours of hundreds and thousands of years have been spent in the attempt to solve this problem. To-day it is more than ever the greatest problem of destiny. No matter how individual persons may reply to the question, how are we to reach a renewal of culture ? (I think I indicated this to some extent) the answer will somehow have to lie in the following direction :—How can we rediscover by a fully human striving man himself, so that in contact with his fellow-man (who in his turn should devote himself fully to the world and his fellows) man may once more find satisfaction in his ethical, social and intellectual life ? This constitutes, I think, the problem dealing with a renewal of our modern culture.

THE RELATIONSHIP OF MAN WITH THE COSMOS

ONLY if it is regarded as a time of trial and testing can anything propitious emerge from the period of grave difficulty through which humanity has been passing. I cannot help thinking to-day of the lectures given in this very town many years ago, before the war, and those of you who have studied what was then said, will have realised that certain definite indications were given of the terrible times ahead. The lectures dealt with the Folk-Souls of the European peoples*, and as a reminder of them—in order, too, that you may realise their purport more clearly—I would like, by way of introduction, to speak of a certain interesting episode.

In the year 1918 I had a conversation in Middle Europe with someone who in the autumn of that year played a brief but significant part in the catastrophic events which were then assuming a particularly menacing form. Those who were able to follow the course of events, however, realised already in the early months of that year that this particular man would be in a key position

---

**The Mission of Folk-Souls.* Eleven lectures, Christiania 7th—17th June, 1910.

when matters came to a point of decision. As I say, I had a talk with him in the month of January, 1918, and in the course of our conversation he spoke of the need for a psychology, for teaching on the subject of the Folk-Souls of the European peoples. The chaos into which humanity was falling would make it essential—so he said—for those who desired to take the lead in public affairs to understand the forces at work in the souls of the peoples of Europe. And he expressed deep regret that there was really no possibility of basing the management of public affairs upon any knowledge of this kind. I answered that I had given lectures on this very subject and I afterwards sent the volume to him, having added a foreword dealing with the situation as it then was—in January, 1918. I tell you this merely in order to indicate the real purport of the lectures. Their aim was to give true guiding lines for counteracting the forces which were leading straight into confusion and chaos. And it was for the same reason that I again made use of them in the year 1918, in the way I have indicated. But it was all quite useless, in spite of the preface dealing with the necessities of the situation that had later arisen, because ripeness of insight was required to understand the strength of the forces leading to decay, and although this ripeness of insight would have been within the reach of many leading men, they were not willing to strive for it.

And it is the same to-day. People are still terribly afraid to envisage, in their true form, the forces that are leading straight into chaos. Instead of facing these forces of decay, they prefer to spin all kinds of fantastic notions, believing that if they take refuge in them, life will go on quite peacefully. But those who will have nothing to do with this kind of thinking and who face the realities of the situation, hold no such belief. Far from it.

Precisely here in Norway destiny made it necessary to speak of the relations between the European Folk-Souls, and indeed I have been speaking of the same theme, with its different ramifications, more or less in detail for many years. I have said more than once that a time will come in European affairs when much will depend upon whether Norway can count among its people, men who will range themselves on the side of true progress and devote their powers to furthering it. The geographical position of Norway renders this imperative and indeed possible. Up here there is a certain detachment from European conditions and this can help many things to ripen. But this ripeness must unfold, gradually, into fruit—into a true and quickened spiritual life.

In the years that have passed since we were last together, you yourselves have had many experiences in connection with the great European War, but only those who lived in the very midst of things were able to realise their full significance. It is difficult to find words of human language that can give any adequate idea of the awful catastrophes. One is tempted to use the word 'senseless' about it all, because nearly everything in the domain of the public affairs of Europe up to the beginning of the twentieth century resulted in some form of senselessness. What went on between the years 1914 and 1918 was a kind of madness, and since then matters have not greatly improved although it may perhaps be said that the senseless actions of the materialistic world are not so outwardly patent as they were during the actual years of the war.

To-day it ought to be realised much more fully than it is, that Europe is bound to come to grief if attention is not turned to the *spiritual foundations* of human life, if merely for purposes of convenience men brush aside all that is said with the intention of helping humanity to emerge from the chaos of anti-spirituality. The fact that my lectures on Folk-Psychology were ignored by one who held a leading position during this period of senseless action, seemed to me to be deeply symptomatic. And it is still the same to-day. Everything is brushed aside by those who have any influence in public life.

It is a pity that the significance of certain words spoken by an Anglo-South African statesman has not been grasped in Europe. The words were not spoken from any great depth, but none the less they indicated a certain feeling for the way in which affairs are shaping at the present time. This statesman said that the focus of world-history has shifted from the North Sea to the Pacific Ocean—that is to say from Europe in general, to the Pacific Ocean. And this too may be added :—That for which, up till now, Europe was a kind of centre, has ceased to exist. We are living in its remains. It has been superseded by great world-affairs as between the East and the West. What is going on now, all unsuspectingly in Washington, is nothing but a feeble stammering, surging up from depths where mighty, unobserved impulses are stirring.

There will be no peace on the Earth until a certain harmony is established between the affairs of East and West, and it must be realised that this harmony has first to be achieved in the realm of the *Spirit*. However glibly people may talk in these difficult times about disarmament and other ' luxuries ' of the kind—for luxuries they are, and nothing more—it will amount to no more than conversation, as long as the Western world fails to discover and bring to light the spirituality that is indeed contained, but allowed to lie fallow in the culture which has been developing since the middle of the fifteenth century. There *is* a store of spiritual treasure in this culture, but it lies fallow.

Science has acquired a magnificent knowledge of the world and we are surrounded on all hands by really marvellous technical achievements. It is all splendid in its way, but it is dead—dead as compared with the great currents of human evolution. And yet in this very death there lies a living spirituality which can shine into the world even more brilliantly than all that was given to man by oriental wisdom—although that must never be belittled. Such a feeling does in truth exist in all unprejudiced observers of life.

We do right to turn to the great wisdom-treasures of the East—of which the Vedas, the wonderful Vedanta philosophy and the like are but mere reflections ; and we are rightly filled with wonder by all that was there revealed from heavenly heights. It has gradually fallen into a certain decadence, but even in the form in which it still lives in the East, it arouses the wonder and admiration of anyone who has a feeling for such things.

In vivid contrast to this there is the purely materialistic culture of the West, of Europe and America. This materialistic culture and its equally materialistic mode of thinking must not be disparaged, yet it is, after all, rather like a hard nutshell—a dying nutshell. But the kernel is still alive and if it can be discovered its radiance will outshine all the glory of oriental wisdom that once poured down to man. Let there be no mistake about it—as long as the dealings of Europeans and Americans with Asia are confined to purely economic and industrial interests, so long will there be distrust in the hearts of Asiatics. People may talk as much as they like about disarmament, about the desirability of ending wars . . . a great war *will* break out between the East and the West, in spite of all disarmament conferences, if the people of Asia cannot perceive something that flows over to them from the *Spirit* of the West. Western spirituality *can* shine over to Asia and if it does, Asia will be able to trust it, because with their own inherent, though somewhat decadent spirituality, the Asiatic peoples will be able to understand what it means. The peace of the world depends upon this, not upon the conversations and discussions now going on among the leaders of outer civilisation.

Everything depends upon insight into the *Spirit* that is lying hidden in European and American culture—the Spirit from which men flee, which for the sake of ease they would fain avoid, but which alone can set the feet of humanity on the path of ascent. People like to put their heads in the sand, saying that things will improve of themselves. No, they will *not*. The hour of a great decision has struck. Either men will resolve to bring forth the spirituality of which I have spoken, or the decline of the West is inevitable. Hopes and fatalistic longings for things to right themselves are of no avail. Once and forever, man has passed into the epoch when he must manipulate his powers out of his own freewill. In other words: *it is for men themselves to decide for or against spirituality*. If the decision is positive, progress will be possible; if not, the doom of the West is sealed and in the wake of dire catastrophes the further evolution of humanity will take a course undreamed of to-day. Those who would strive for true insight into these matters should not, nay dare not, neglect the study of the life of soul in mankind at large and in the different peoples, especially of East and West.

In these preliminary remarks I have tried to convey that if in this particular corner of Europe, qualities to which the Scandinavian Spirit is peculiarly adapted, can be unfolded, insight can ripen and work fruitfully upon the rest of the Western world. Indeed it will only be possible for a spiritual Movement to be taken seriously when with inner understanding men are prepared to ascribe to it a mission of the kind here indicated.

Modern thought studies everything in the universe beyond the Earth in terms of mathematics and mechanics. We look at the stars through telescopes, examine their substance by means of the spectroscope and the like, reducing these observations to rules of calculation, and we have finally arrived at a great system of 'world-machinery' in which our Earth is placed like a wheel. Fantastic notions are evolved about the habitableness of other planets, but no great significance is attached to them because we fall back upon mathematical formulae when it is a question of speaking of extra-terrestrial space. Man has gradually come to feel himself living on Earth just as a mole might feel in his mound during the winter. There is an idea that the Earth is rather like a tiny mole-hill in the universe. There is also a tendency to look back with a certain superciliousness to 'primitive' periods of culture, for instance to the culture of ancient Egypt, when men did not speak of the great mechancial processes in the Universe but of divine *Beings* outside in space and beyond space—Beings to whom man was known to be related just as he is related to the beings of the three kingdoms of Nature on Earth.

The ancient Egyptian traced the origin of the spirit and soul of man to the higher Hierarchies, to supersensible worlds, just as he traced the origin of his material, bodily nature to the mineral, plant and animal kingdoms. In our age, people speak of what is beyond the Earth out of a kind of weak and ever-weakening faith that much prefers to avoid scientific scrutiny. Science speaks only of a great system of world-machinery which can be expressed in terms of mathematics. Earthly existence has finally come to be regarded as confined within the walls of a little mole-hill in the universe.

Yet there is a profound truth, namely this: When man loses the heavens, he loses *himself*. By far the most important elements of man's being belong to the universe beyond the Earth and if he loses sight of this universe he loses sight of his own true being. He wanders over the Earth without knowing what kind of being he really is. He knows, but even then only from tradition, that the word 'man' applies to him, that this name was once given to him as a being who stands upright in contrast to the quadruped animals. But his scientific view of the world and technical culture no longer help him to discover the true content of his name, for that must be sought in the universe beyond the Earth, and this universe is considered to be nothing but a great system of machinery. Man has lost himself; he has no longer any insight into his true nature.

A feeling of sadness cannot but overtake us when we realise that the heights of culture to which the West has risen since the middle of the fifteenth century have led man to wrench himself from his true nature and to live on the Earth divested of soul and spirit.

In the lecture to educationists yesterday, I said that we are prone to speak of only one aspect —and even that merely from tradition—of the eternal being of man. We speak of eternity beyond *death* but not of the eternity stretching beyond *birth*, nor of how the human being has descended from spiritual worlds into material, physical existence on the Earth. And so we really have no word which corresponds, at the other pole, to 'deathlessness' or immortality. We do not speak of 'unborn-ness' (*Ungeborenheit*) but until it becomes a natural matter of course to speak of deathlessness *and* unborn-ness, the true being of man will never be understood.

The meaning attaching to the word 'deathlessness' nowadays is very far from what it was in times when men also spoke of 'unborn-ness.' Innumerable sermons are preached to-day, and with a certain subjective honesty, on the eternal nature of the human soul. But get to the root of these sermons and see if you can discover their fundamental trend. They speculate strongly upon the *egotism* of human beings, upon the fact that man longs for immortality because his egotism makes the idea of annihilation at death distasteful to him. Think about all that is said along these lines and you will realise that the sermons are directed to the egotism in the members of orthodox congregations. When it comes to the question of pre-existence, of the life before *birth*, it is not possible to reckon with human egotism. Nothing in the egotistical souls of men arises in response to teaching about the life before birth, because no interest is taken in it. The attitude is more or less this : If indeed there was a life before birth, we are experiencing a continuation of it. One thing is certain ! we are in existence *now*. What, then, is the object of speaking of what went before ? It is, in short, only egotism that makes man hold fast to the teaching that death does not bring annihilation. And so, in speaking of the life before birth, one has to appeal to *selflessness*, to the quality that is the very reverse of egotism. It is, of course, quite right to speak also of the life after death, although the appeal there is to the egotism of the soul. That is the great difference.

It is clear from this that egotism has laid hold of the very depths of the human soul. The anathema placed upon the doctrine of pre-existence is a consequence of the egotism in the soul. It behoves all who are earnest in their striving for spiritual insight to understand these things. Man must find himself again and be true to the laws of his innermost being. Interest must be awakened in the *whole* nature of man, instead of being confined to his outer, physical sheaths. But this end cannot be achieved until man is regarded as belonging not only to the Earth—which is conceived as a little mole-hill—but to the whole Cosmos, until it is realised that between death and a new birth he passes through the world of stars to which here on Earth he can only gaze upwards from below. And the living essence, the soul and the spirit of the world of stars must be known once again.

The first thing we observe about a human being is his outer, physical structure, but the essential principle, namely its *form*, is generally disregarded. Form, after all, is the most fundamental principle so far as physical man is concerned. Now when we embark upon a theme like this—which has been dealt with from so many angles in other lectures—it will be obvious at once that only brief indications can be given. Knowing something of the spiritual teachings of Anthroposophy, however, you will realise that what I shall now say is drawn from a deeper knowledge of the world and is something more than a series of unsubstantiated statements.

The human form is a most marvellous structure. Think, to begin with, of the *head*. In all its parts, the head is a copy of the universe. Its form is spherical, the spherical form being modified at the base in order to provide for the articulation of other organs and systems. The essential form of the head, however, is a copy of the spherical form of the universe, as you can discover if you study the basic formation of the embryo.

Linked to the head-structure is another formation which still retains something of the spherical form, although this is not so immediately apparent—I mean the *chest-structure*. Try to conceive this chest-structure imaginatively; it is as if a spherical form had been compressed and then released again, as if a sphere had undergone an organic metamorphosis.

Finally, in the limb-structures, we can discover hardly anything of the primal, embryonic form of man. Spiritual Science alone will make us alive to the fact that the limb-structures too, still reveal certain final traces of a spherical form although this is not very obvious in their outer shape.

When we study the threefold human form in its relation to the Cosmos, we can say that man is shaped and moulded by cosmic forces but these forces work upon him in many different ways. The changing position of the Sun in the zodiacal constellations through the various epochs has been taken as an indication of the different forces which pour down to man from the world of the fixed stars. Even our mechanistic astronomy to-day speaks of the fact that the Sun rises in a particular constellation at the vernal equinox, that in the course of the coming centuries it will pass through others, that during the day it passes through certain constellations and during the night through others. These and many other things are said, but there is no conscious knowledge of man's relationship to the universe beyond the Earth. It is little known, for example, that when the Sun is shining upon the Earth at the vernal equinox from the constellation of Aries, the solar forces streaming down into human beings in a particular part of the Earth are modified by the influences proceeding from the region in the heaven of fixed stars represented by the constellation of Aries. Neither is there any knowledge of the fact that these forces are peculiarly adapted to work upon the human *head* in such a way indeed, that during earthly life man can unfold a certain faculty of self-observation, self-knowledge and consciousness of his own Ego.

During the Greek epoch, as you know, the Sun stood in the constellation of Aries at the vernal equinox. In the Greek epoch, therefore, Western peoples were particularly subject to the Aries forces. The fact of being subject to the Aries forces makes it possible for the head of man to develop in such a way that Ego-consciousness, a faculty for self-contemplation, unfolds.

Even when the history of the zodiacal symbols is discussed to-day, there is not always knowledge of the essentials. Historical traditions speak of the zodiacal symbols—Aries, Taurus, Gemini, and so forth. In old calendars we frequently find the symbol of Aries, but very few people indeed realise the point of greatest significance, which is that the Ram is depicted with his head looking *backwards*. This image was intended to indicate that the Aries forces influence man in the direction of inwardness—for the Ram does not look forward, nor out into the wide world—he looks backwards, upon himself; he contemplates his own being. This is full of meaning. Once again, and this time in full consciousness not with the instinctive—clairvoyance of olden times—once again we must press forward to this cosmic wisdom, to the knowledge that the forces of the human head are developed essentially through the forces of Aries, Taurus, Gemini and Cancer, whereas the forces of the chest-structure are subject to those of the four middle constellations—Leo, Virgo, Libra, Scorpio. The human head receives it's form from the inworking forces of Aries, Taurus, Gemini and Cancer—forces which must be conceived as radiating from above downwards, whereas the zodiacal forces to which the chest-organisation of man is essentially subject (Leo, Virgo, Libra, Scorpio), work *laterally*.

The other four constellations lie beneath the Earth; their forces work *through* the Earth, not directly down upon it as those of Aries, Taurus,

Gemini, Cancer, nor laterally as those of Leo, Virgo, Libra, Scorpio, but from *below upwards*. They work upon the limb-structures, and in such a way that the spherical form cannot remain intact. These are the constellations which in the instinctive consciousness of olden times, man envisaged as working up from beneath the Earth. When the constellations lie beneath the Earth, they work upon the limb-structures. And in days of yore there was consciousness of the fact that the forces by which the limbs are given shape are connected with these particular constellations.

The spherical form of the head—this was known to be connected with Aries, Taurus, Gemini, Cancer; the forces working in the limbs were also conceived of as fourfold. Now it must be remembered that this knowledge was the outcome of ancient clairvoyance, hence the terms employed are concerned with conditions of life prevailing in those days. Thus, according to the wisdom of the stars, a man might be a hunter— one who shoots; the constellation which stimulated the corresponding activity in his limbs, making him a hunter, received the name of Sagittarius, the archer. Or again, a man might be a shepherd, concerned with the care of animals in general. This is implied in Capricorn, as it is called nowadays. In the true symbol, however, there is a fish-tail form. The Capricorn man is one who has charge of animals, in contrast to the hunter, the Sagittarius man.

The third constellation of this group is Aquarius, the water-carrier. But think of the ancient symbol. The true picture of this constellation is a man walking over hard soil, fertilising or watering it from a water-vessel. He represents those who are concerned with agriculture—husbandmen. This was the third calling in ancient times when there was instinctive knowledge of these things : huntsman, shepherd, husbandman.

The fourth calling was that of a mariner, In very early times, ships were built in the form of a fish, and later on we often find a dolphin's head at the prow of vessels. This is what underlies the symbol of Pisces—two fish forms intertwined —representing ships trading together. This is symbolical of the fourth calling which is bound up with activities of the limbs—the merchant or trader.

We have thus heard how the human form and figure originate from the Cosmos. The head is spherical ; here man is directly exposed to the forces of the heavens of the fixed stars or their representatives the zodiacal circle. Then, working laterally, there are the forces present in the chest-organisation which only contains the human figure in an eclipsed and hidden form— Leo, Virgo, Libra, Scorpio. And lastly there are the forces which do not work directly but by a roundabout way, via the earthly activities, through the influence upon man's calling. (For example, the archer—Sagittarius—is also portrayed as a kind of centaur, half horse, half man, and so forth).

Again in our time we must strive for a fully conscious realisation of man's place in the Cosmos. The form and shape of his physical body are given by the Cosmos. The upper part of his structure is a product of the Cosmos; the lower part a product of the Earth. The Earth covers those constellations which have a definite connection with his activities in life. Not until man's connection with the whole Cosmos is thus recognised and acknowledged will it be possible to understand the mysteries of the human form and its relation to earthly activities. And at the very outset the human form leads us to the zodiacal constellations.

This teaches us that to work as a husbandman, for instance, is by no means without significance in life. In the following lectures we shall hear how these things apply in modern times, but we shall not understand them until we realise that just as in earthly life between birth and death, man belongs to the powers of the Earth, so between death and a new birth he belongs to the Heavens; the powers of Heaven shape his head and it is left to the forces of Earth to shape and mould his limbs.

In the same way too, we may study man's stages or forms of *life*. For think of it—in the life of man there are also the same two poles. There is the head-life and the life that expresses itself in his activities, through the limbs more particularly. Between these two poles lies that part of his being which manifests in the rhythms of breathing and the circulation of the blood. At the one extreme we find the head-organisation; at the other, the limb-organisation.

The head represents the dying part of man's being, for the head is perpetually involved in death. Life is only possible because through the whole of earthly life, forces are continually pouring from the metabolic process to the head. If the head were to unfold merely its own natural forces, they would be the forces of death. But to this dying we owe the fact that we can think and be conscious beings. The moment the pure life-forces flow in excess to the head, consciousness is prone to be lost. Basically speaking, then, life makes for a *dimming* of consciousness; death pouring into life makes for a *lighting-up* of consciousness.* If only very little of what is rightly located in the stomach, for example, were to pass up to the head, the head would be without consciousness—like the stomach. Man owes the consciousness of his head merely to the circumstance that the head is *not* permeated with life in the same way as the stomach. Lowered consciousness means that the forces of nourishment and of growth are acting with excessive strength in the head. On the one side, man is a dying being; on the other, a being who is continually coming to birth. The dying part—which, however, determines the existence of consciousness—is subject, in the main, to the forces working down upon the Earth from the outer planets: Saturn, Jupiter, Mars. That man is an integral part of the universe is not only due to the working of the fixed stars, but also to the working of the planetary spheres.

Saturn, Jupiter, Mars—the so-called outer planets—contain the forces which work chiefly

---

*See *Fundamentals of Therapy*, by Rudolf Steiner and Dr. Ita Wegman, Chapter I, pages 14—15.

towards the pole of *consciousness* in man. The forces of the inner planets—Venus, Mercury, Moon— work into his metabolic system and limb-structures. The Sun itself stands in the middle and is mainly associated with the rhythmic system.

Moreover the three first-mentioned are the three stages of life which rather represent the damping-down and suppression of life which is necessary for the sake of consciousness. Through this, we, in our earthly life, are liker to heaven, related to more distant planetary realms beyond. On the other hand, through the essentially thriving principle of life itself in us—that is through the forces of metabolism, the motor forces of the limbs—we are related to the nearer planets : Mercury, Venus and Moon. The Moon, after all, is directly connected with the most thriving, with the most rampant life of all in man, namely the forces of reproduction.

When we study the human *form*, we are led to the spheres of the fixed stars, that is to say, to their representatives, the zodiacal constellations. When we study the *life* of man, to discover where it is a more thriving and where a more declining life, we are led to the planetary spheres.

In the same way we can study man's being of soul and of spirit. This shall be done in the following lectures. To-day I only wanted to indicate very briefly that it must become possible for man once again to regard himself not merely as an earthly being, connecting his form and his life simply and solely with earthly forces of heredity, digestion, the influences of autumn, spring, wind, weather and the like. He must learn to relate both his life and his form to the universe *beyond* the Earth. He must find what lies beyond the earthly realm—and then he will discover his true being, he will find *himself*.

It would augur dire misfortune for the progress of Western humanity if the conception of the Cosmos as a great system of machinery to which the scientific view of the world since the middle of last century has led, were to remain, and if man were to wander on Earth knowing nothing of his true being. His true being has its origin and home in the Universe beyond the Earth, therefore he can know nothing of himself if he sees only what is earthly and thinks that what is beyond the Earth can be explained in terms of mathematics and mechanics. In deed and truth, man can only find himself when he realises his connection with the universe beyond the Earth and incorporates its forces into his moral and social life—indeed this must be, if moral and social life are to thrive. No real wisdom can arise in moral and social life unless a link is forged with cosmic wisdom. And that is why it has been imperative to infuse something of Anthroposophy into the domain of moral and social life too, for we believe that these impulses can lead away from the forces of decline to the forces of upward progress.

THE SOUL LIFE OF MAN IN RELATION TO HIGHER WORLDS

WE have heard how in accordance with anthroposophical knowledge, the being of man must be viewed in relation to the whole universe. We considered the human form and figure and its relation to the fixed stars, or rather to the representative of the fixed stars—the Zodiac. We heard how certain forces proceed from the constellations of these stars when combined with the Sun forces, and how the shape and structure of the human head and the organs connected with it, are related to the upper constellations of the Zodiac: Aries, Taurus, Gemini, Cancer. The structure of the human chest-organisation is connected with the middle constellations: Leo, Virgo, Libra, Scorpio. Finally the metabolic-and-limb system is connected with the lower constellations: Sagittarius, Capricorn, Aquarius, Pisces—that is to say with their forces when they are, in a sense, covered by the Earth. So that we can say: The fixed stars—for the Zodiac is only the representative of the fixed stars—work upon the human *form* and *structure*.

The planetary spheres work upon man's stages or forms of *life*. It must indeed be quite clear to us that man has various kinds of life in him. We should not be able to think, the head would not be an organ of thought, if life were as rampant there as it is in the metabolic system, for example. When metabolism becomes too strong in the head, consciousness is extinguished; we lose our consciousness of self.

From this it may be concluded that for consciousness, for mental presentation, a damped-down, suppressed life, a declining life is necessary; while a thriving life, vehement and intense, is necessary for what works more from out of the unconscious, to become *will*.

We have therefore among the various stages of life some which tend towards self-extinction, and some in which strong, intense organic activity manifests, as in a child, in whom thought is not yet operating. We have this child-like life continually within us; but into this child-like life, the life that is involved in a gradual process of death, inserts itself.

These different stages of life are connected with the planetary spheres. Whereas the fixed stars work in man through his physical forces, the planetary spheres work through his *etheric* forces. The planetary spheres, therefore, work upon man in a more delicate way. But the human physical body has already received its form, its shape from the fixed stars, not from anything earthly; and its stages of life from the planetary spheres.

We have thus considered the *form* of man's physical body, the *life-stages* of his ether-body. We can now proceed to consider his life of soul-and-spirit. But here our mode of study must be different. What is it that our physical and our ether-body provide for us in waking life?

They provide what we perceive through our senses and what we can work over in our thoughts. We are only really *awake* in our acts of sense-perception and when we work over them in thought.

On the other hand, consider the life of *feeling*. It is obvious, even to superficial study, that feeling does not indicate a state of awakeness as complete as that of thinking and sense-perception. When we wake in the morning and become aware of the colours and sounds of the outside world, when we are conscious of the conditions of warmth around us, we are fully awake and then, in our thoughts, we work over what is transmitted by the senses. But when feelings rise up from the soul, it cannot be said that we are *conscious* in them to the same extent. Feelings link themselves with sense-perceptions. One sense-impression pleases us, another displeases us. Feelings also intermingle with our thoughts. But if we compare the pictures we experience in dreams with what we experience in our feelings, then the connection between dream-life and the life of feeling is clearly noticeable.

Dreams have to be grasped by the waking life of thought if they are to be valued and understood aright. But feelings too must be observed, as it were, by our thought-life if we are to understand them. In our feelings we are, in reality, *dreaming*. When we dream, we dream in pictures. When we are awake, we dream in our feelings. And in our *will* we are asleep, even when fully awake. When we raise an arm, when we do this or that, we can *perceive* what movements the arm or hand is making, but we do not know *how* the power of the will operates in the organism. We know as little about that as about the conditions prevailing from the time we fall asleep until we wake up. In our willing, in our actions, we are asleep, while in our sense-perceptions and our thoughts, we are awake. So we are not only asleep during the night; we are asleep, in part of our being, during waking life too. In our will we are asleep and in our feelings we dream. What we experience during actual sleep is withdrawn from our consciousness. But in essence, the same is true of feeling and willing. It is therefore obviously important to realise what it is that the human being experiences in these realms of which ordinary life is quite unaware.

You know from many anthroposophical lectures that from the time of going to sleep until that of waking, the Ego and astral body are outside the physical body and the ether-body. Now it may be of very great importance to learn about just those experiences which the Ego and the astral body pass through from the time of falling asleep to that of waking up. When we are awake, we are confronted by sense-perceptions of the material world. To a certain extent we reach out and encounter them; but with our sense-perceptions, our waking thoughts, we reach no further than the surface of things.

Of course someone may object, saying that he *can* get further than the surface of things, that if he cuts a piece of wood which is there before him as a sense-perception, then he has penetrated inside it. That is a fallacy, however, for if you cut a piece of wood, you have again only a surface, and if you cut the two pieces again, still you have only surfaces; and if you were to get right to the molecules and atoms, again you would have only surfaces. You do not reach what may be called the inner essence of things, for that lies beyond the realm of sense-perception. Sense-perceptions can be conceived as a tapestry spread out around us. What lies this side of the tapestry we perceive with our senses; what lies on the other side of the tapestry we do not perceive with the senses. We are in this world of sense from the time we wake up until we fall asleep. Our soul is filled with the impressions made upon us by this world of sense. Now when we pass into sleep, we are not in the world this side of the senses, we are then in reality *inside* things, we are on the *other* side of the tapestry of sense-perceptions. But in his earthly consciousness, man knows nothing of this and he dreams of all sorts of things lying beyond the realm of sense-perception. He dreams of molecules, of atoms; but they are only dreams—dreams of his waking consciousness. He invents molecules, atoms and the like, and believes them to be realities. But study any description of atoms, even the most recent . . . you will find nothing but minute objects which are described according to the pattern of what is experienced from the surface of things. It is all a tissue woven from the experiences of waking consciousness on this side of the tapestry of sense.

But when we fall asleep, we emerge from the world of sense and penetrate to the other side.

And whereas we experience Nature here with our waking thoughts, in yonder world, from the time of falling asleep until the time of waking, we live in the world of Spirit, that world of Spirit through which we also pass before birth and after death. In his earthly development, however, man is so constituted that his consciousness is extinguished when he passes beyond the world of sense; his consciousness is not forceful enough to penetrate to the spiritual world. But what Spiritual Science calls Imagination, Inspiration, Intuition—these three forms of supersensible cognition—give us knowledge of what lies on the other side of the tapestry of sense. And what we discover first, is the lowest stage of the world of the Hierarchies.

When we wake from sleep we pass over into the world of animals, plants, minerals—the three kingdoms of Nature belonging to the world of sense. When we fall asleep, we pass beyond the world of sense, we are transported into the realm of the first rank of Beings above man—the Angels. And from the time of falling asleep until waking, we are connected with the Being who is allotted to man as his own Angel, just as through our eyes and ears we are connected with the three kingdoms of Nature here in the world of sense. Even if at first we have no consciousness of this connection with the world of the Angels, it is nevertheless there. This connection extends into our astral body.

If, living in our astral body during sleep, we were suddenly to wake up, we should contact the world of the Angels, in the first place the

Angel who is connected with our own life, just as here in the earthly world we are in contact with animals, plants, and minerals.

Now even in the earthly world, in the world of sense, if a man is attentive and deliberately trains his thinking, he sees much more than when he is unobservant and hasty. His connection with the three kingdoms of Nature can be intimate or superficial. And it is the same with regard to the world of spiritual Beings. But in the world of spiritual Beings, different conditions prevail.

A man whose thoughts are entirely engrossed in the material world, who never desires to rise above it, or to acquaint himself with moral ideas extending beyond the merely utilitarian, who has no desire to experience true human love, who in his waking life has no devotion to the Divine-Spiritual world—on falling asleep, such a man has no forces which enable him to come into contact with his Angel. Whenever we fall asleep, this Angel is waiting as it were for the idealistic feelings and thoughts which come with us, and the more we bring, the more intimate becomes our relation to the Angel while we are asleep. And so throughout our life, by means of what we cultivate over and above material interests, we garner, in our waking life, forces whereby our relation to the Angel becomes more and more intimate.

When we die, all sense-perceptions fall away. The outer world can no longer make any impression upon us, for this must be done via the senses, and the senses pass away with the body. In like manner, the thinking that is connected with sense-perception is extinguished, for its realm is the ether-body. This ether-body only remains with us for a few days after death. We see it at first as a tableau—a tableau which under certain circumstances can be glimpsed during life but which will inevitably arise before us after death.

This ether-tissue dissolves away into the universe, just as the ordinary thoughts acquired from the world of sense pass away from us. They do not remain. All purely utilitarian thoughts, all thoughts connected with the material world, drift away from us when we pass through the Gate of Death. But the idealistic thoughts and feelings, the pure human love, the religious feelings which have arisen in our waking life and have united us with our Angel, these accompany us when we pass through death.

This has a very important consequence during the period lying between death and a new birth. Even during earthly life we are connected with the higher Hierarchies and it is correct to say that when we fall asleep and our idealistic experiences reach to the Angel, this Angel is in turn connected with the Archangels, the Archangels with the Archai, and so on. Our existence continues in a rich and abundant world of Spirit. But this spiritual world has no special significance for us between birth and death. This world of the higher Hierarchies acquires its real significance for us when it becomes our environment between death and a new birth. The more we have delivered over to our Angel, the more *conscious* life is this Angel able to infuse into us after death when we are beings of soul-and-spirit, the more gifts are bestowed by the Hierarchies upon the conscious life of soul. What our Angel unfolds, together with the higher Hierarchies (that is to say, what the Beings of the First Hierarchy unfold together with higher Hierarchies *through* our Angel) is for our consciousness in the spiritual world between death and rebirth what our eyes and ears are in the physical world. And the more idealistic thoughts and feelings, human love and piety we have brought to our Angel, the clearer does our consciousness become.

Now between death and a new birth there comes a time when the Angel has a definite task in connection with us. The Angel has now to achieve a more intimate relation with the hierarchy of the Archangels than was formerly the case. I have described the time through which man lives between death and a new birth from many different points of view, notably in the Lecture-Course given in Vienna in 1914, entitled *The Inner Nature of Man and the Life between Death and a new Birth*. I will now describe certain other aspects.

When a somewhat lengthy period has elapsed after death, the important moment comes when the Angel must as it were deliver up to the Archangels what he has received from us through the 'idealistic' experiences described. It is as though man were placed before the world of the Archangels, who can then receive these experiences he has unfolded in his soul and Spirit during his life between birth and death. There are great differences among human souls living between death and a new birth. In our epoch there are persons who have brought very little in the way of idealistic thoughts and feelings, of human love, of piety, when the time comes for the Angel to pass on to the Archangel for the purposes of cosmic evolution, what has been carried through death. This activity which unfolds between the Angel and the Archangel must, under all circumstances, take place. But there is a great difference, dependent upon whether we are able to follow consciously, by means of the experiences described, what takes place between the Angels and the Archangels or whether we only live through it in a dull, dim state, as must be the lot of human beings whose consciousness has been purely materialistic. It is not quite accurate to say that the experiences of such human beings are dull or dim. It is perhaps better to say : they experience these happenings in such a way that they feel continually rejected by a world into which they ought to be received, they feel continually chilled by a world which should receive them with warmth. For man should be received with loving sympathy into the world of the Archangels at this important moment of time ; he should be received with warmth. And then he will be led in the right way towards what I have called in one of my Mystery Plays : " The Midnight Hour of Existence."

Man is led by the Archangels to the realm of the Archai where his life is interwoven with that of all the higher Hierarchies, for through the Archai he is brought into relation with all the higher Hierarchies and receives from their realms the impulse to descend to the Earth once again. The power is given him to work as a being of soul-and-spirit, to work in what is provided, later on, in material form, by the stream of heredity.

Before the Midnight Hour of Existence man has become more and more estranged from earthly existence, he has been growing more and more into the spiritual world—either being received lovingly (in the sense described above) by the spiritual world, being drawn to it with warmth, or being repelled, chilled by it. But when the Midnight Hour of Existence has passed, man begins gradually to long for earthly life and once again, during the second part of his journey, he encounters the world of the Archangels. It is really so : Between death and a new birth, man ascends, first to the world of the Angels, Archangels, Archai, and then once again descends ; and after the world of the Archai his most important contact is with the world of the Archangels.

And now comes another important point in the life between death and a new birth. In a man who has brought through death no idealistic thoughts or feelings, no human love or true piety, something of the soul-and-spirit has perished as a result of the antipathy and chilling reception meted out by the higher world. A man who now again approaches the realm of the Archangels in the right way has received into him the power to work effectively in his subsequent life on Earth, to make proper use of his body ; a man who has not brought such experiences with him will be imbued by the Angels with a longing for earthly life which remains more unconscious. A very great deal depends upon this. Upon it depends to what people, to what language—mother-tongue —the man descends in his forthcoming earthly existence. This urge towards a particular people, a particular mother-tongue may have been implanted in him deeply and inwardly or more superficially. So that on his descent a man is either permeated with deep and inward love for what will become his mother-tongue, or he enters more automatically into what he will have to express later on through his organs of speech.

It makes a great difference in which of these two ways a man has been destined for the language that will be his in the coming earthly life. He who before his earthly life, during his second passage through the realm of the Angels, can be permeated with a really inward love for his mother-tongue, assimilates it as though it were part of his very being. He becomes one with it. This love is absolutely natural to him; it is a love born of the soul; he grows into his language and race as into a natural home. If however a man has grown into it the other way during the descent to his next earthly life, he will arrive on the Earth loving his language merely out of instinct and lower impulses. Lacking the true, inward love for his language and his people, he will be prone to an aggressive patriotism connected with his bodily existence. It makes a great difference whether we grow into race and language with the tranquil, pure love of one who unites himself inwardly with his folk and language, or whether we grow into them more automatically, and out of passions and instincts express love for our folk and our language. The former conditions never come to expression in chauvinism or a superficial and aggressive form of patriotism. A true and inward love for race and language expresses itself naturally, and is thoroughly consistent with real and universal human love. Feeling for internationalism or cosmopolitanism is never stultified by this inner love for a language and people. When, however, a man grows into his language more automatically, when through his instincts and impulses he develops an over-fervid, organic, animal-like love for language and people, false nationalism and chauvinism arise, with their external emphasis upon race and nationality.

At the present time especially, it is necessary to study from the standpoint of life between death and a new birth what we encounter in the outer world in our life between birth and death. For the way we come down into race and language through the stream of heredity, through birth, depends upon how we encounter, for the second time, the realm of the Archangels.

Those who try to understand life to-day from the spiritual vantage-point, know that the experience arising in the period between death and a new birth when man comes for the second time into the realm of the Angels, is very important. All over the Earth to-day the peoples are adopting a false attitude to nationality, race and language, and much of what has arisen in the catastrophe of the second decade of the twentieth century in the evolution of the Western people, is only explicable when studied from such points of view.

He who studies life to-day in the light of anthroposophical Spiritual Science must assume that in former earthly lives many men became more and more deeply entangled in materialism. You all know that, normally, the period between death and a new birth is lengthy. But especially in the present phase of evolution, there are many men whose life between their last death and their present birth was only short, and in their former earthly life they had little human love or idealism. Already in the former earthly life their interests were merely utilitarian. And as a result, in their second contact with the realm of the Angels between death and a new birth, the seeds were laid for all that arises to-day in such an evil form in the life of the West.

We shall have realised that man can only be understood as a spatial being when it is known that his form and structure derive from the realm of the fixed stars and his life-stages from the planetary spheres. As a spatial being, man draws the forces that are active in him, not only from the Earth but from the whole Cosmos. Now just as it is necessary to go beyond what is earthly in order to understand man as a spatial being, so it is necessary to go beyond life between birth and death in order to understand social life, racial life on the Earth.

When we carefully observe the life of to-day we find that although men claim their right to freedom so vociferously, they are, in reality, inwardly unfree. There is no truly free life in the activities which nowadays manifest such obvious forces of decline ; instincts and lower impulses are the cause of the misery in social life. And when this is perceived we are called upon to understand it.

Just as a second meeting with the Archangels takes place, so when man once again approaches earthly life, he enters into a more intimate union with his Angel. But at first he is somewhat withdrawn from the realm of the Angels. As long as he is in the realm of the Archangels, his Angel too is more strongly bound with this realm. Man lives as it were among the higher Hierarchies and as he draws near to a new birth he is entrusted more and more to the realm of the Angels who then lead him through the world of the Elements, through fire, air, water and earth, to the stream of heredity. His Angel leads him to physical existence on Earth. His Angel can make him into a man who is in a position to act freely, out of the depths of his soul-and-spirit, if all the conditions described have been fulfilled by the achievements of a former earthly life.

But the Angel is not able to lead a man to a truly free life, if he has had to be united automatically with his language and his race. In such a case the individual life also becomes unfree. This lack of freedom shows itself in the following way. Instead of forming free concepts, such a man merely thinks *words*. He becomes unfree because all his thinking is absorbed in words. This is a fundamental characteristic of modern men.

Earthly life in its historical development, especially in its present state, cannot be understood unless we also turn with the eyes of soul, to the life which runs its course between death and a new birth, to the world of soul-and-spirit.

To understand the human *form*, we must turn to the heaven of the fixed stars; to understand the stages of *life* in man we must turn to the planetary spheres. If we wish to understand man's life of *soul-and-spirit*, we must not confine our attention to the life between birth and death, for as we have seen, this life of soul-and-spirit is rooted in the world of the higher Hierarchies and belongs to the higher Hierarchies just as the physical body and ether-body of man belong to the physical and etheric worlds.

Again, if we wish to understand thinking, feeling and willing, then we must not merely confine our attention to man's relation to the world of sense. Thinking, feeling and willing are the forces through which the *soul* develops. We are carried as it were through the Gate of Death by our idealistic thoughts—by what love and religious devotion have implanted in these thoughts. Our first meeting with the Archangels depends upon how we have ennobled our thinking and permeated it with idealism. But when we have passed through the Midnight Hour of Existence, our thinking dies away. It is this thinking which now, after the Midnight Hour of Existence, is re-moulded and elaborated for the next earthly life. And the forces which permeate our physical organs of thinking in the coming earthly life are shaped by our former thinking. The forces working in the human head are not merely forces of the present life. They are the forces which have worked over into this life from thinking as it was in the last life, and give rise to the form of the brain.

On the other hand, it is the *will* which, at the second meeting with the Archangels, plays its special part in man's life of soul-and-spirit. And it is the will which then, in the next life on Earth, lays hold of the limb-and-metabolic organism. When we enter through birth into earthly life, it is the will which determines the fitness or inadequacy of the limbs and the metabolic processes.

Within the head we really have a physical mirror-image of the thoughts evolved in the previous life. In the forces of the metabolism and limbs we have the working of the newly acquired forces of will which, at the second meeting with the Archangels, are incorporated into us as I have described—either in such a way that they are inwardly active in the life of soul, or operate automatically.

Those who realise how this present life which generates such forces of decline in humanity of the West, has taken shape, will look with the greatest interest towards what was active in man between death and a new birth during the period of existence preceding this present earthly life. And what they can learn from this will fill them with the impulse—now that the dire consequences of materialism are becoming apparent in the life of the peoples—to give men who already in their last incarnation were too materialistic, that stimulus which can lead once again to a deepening of inner life, to free spiritual activity, to a really intimate and natural relation to language and race which does not in any way run counter to internationalism or cosmopolitanism.

But first and foremost our thinking must be permeated with real spirituality. In the Spirit of modern man, there are, in reality, only thoughts. When man speaks to-day of his Spirit, he is actually speaking only of his thoughts, of his more or less abstract thinking. What we need is to be filled with Spirit, the living Spirit belonging to the world lying between death and a new birth. In respect of his form, his stages of life, his nature of soul-and-spirit, man must regard himself as belonging to a world which lies *outside* the earthly sphere; then he will be able to bring what is right and good into earthly life.

We know how the Spiritual in man is gradually absorbed by other domains of earthly existence, by political life, by economic life. What is needed is a *free and independent spiritual life;* only thereby can man be permeated with real spirituality, with spiritual substance, not merely with thoughts about this or that. Anthroposophy must therefore be prepared to work for the liberation of the spiritual life. If this spiritual life does not stand upon its own foundations, man will become more and more a dealer in abstractions, He will not be able to permeate his being with living Spirit, but only with abstract Spirit.

When a man here, in physical life, passes through the Gate of Death, his corpse is committed to the Earth, or to the Elements. His true being is no longer within this physical corpse. When a man passes through birth in such a way that through the processes described he has become an 'automaton' in his relation to his nation, language and conduct—then his living thinking, his living will, his living nature of soul-and-spirit *die* when he is born into the physical world and within physical existence become the corpse of the Divine Being of soul-and-spirit.

Our abstract, rationalistic thinking is verily a corpse of the soul-and-spirit. Just as the real human being is no longer within the physical corpse, so we have in abstract thinking, a life of soul that is devoid of Spirit—really only the corpse of the Divine-spiritual. Man stands to-day at a critical point where he must resolve to receive the spiritual world once again, in order that he may pour new life into the abstract thinking that is a corpse of the Divine-Spiritual, opening the way for instincts, impulses and automatism.

What I said at the end of my lecture to students here* is deeply true : If he is to pass from a decline to a real ascent, man must overcome the abstraction which, like a corpse of the soul is present in the intellectualistic and rationalistic thinking of to-day.

An awakening of the soul and spirit—that is what is needed ! The social life of the present day points clearly to the necessity for such an awakening. Anthroposophy has indeed an eternal task in regard to that living principle in man which must continue beyond all epochs of time. But Anthroposophy has also a task to fulfil for the present age, namely to wean man from externalisation, from the tendency to paralyse and kill

---
**On the Reality of Higher Worlds.* 25th November, 1921.

the Divine-Spiritual within him. Anthroposophy must bring back this Divine-Spiritual life. Man must learn to regard himself not merely as an earthly but as a heavenly being, realising that his earthly life can only be conducted aright if the forces of heavenly existence, of the existence between death and a new birth, are brought down into this earthly life.

THE DEVELOPMENT OF CHRISTIAN LIFE IN EUROPE: THE MISSION OF THE SCANDINAVIAN PEOPLES

THE two previous lectures dealt with important questions relating to the nature and destiny of man. We heard that the human physical body and ether-body are not connected merely with the external world perceived by the senses and that this bodily nature of man can only be understood aright when we also recognise its relation with the Zodiac. And we then tried to understand how the heaven of the fixed stars and the planetary spheres work upon what lies within the outer covering of man, shaping and imbuing it with life. In the last lecture we also heard how the inner, spiritual core of man's being is related to the world of the higher Hierarchies. It was indicated that this connection with the world of the higher Hierarchies becomes especially noticeable when we observe how in his physical life on Earth, man can achieve union with the spiritual world through morality, religious devotion and love for his fellow-men ; in this way he enables his Guardian Angel so to order his descent at the end of his life between death and a new birth that he again acquires the full power of individuality and is able, as a free individual, to take hold of his human nature. We also heard that if a man has not established this relation to the spiritual world in some incarnation, his link with his nation, for example, is of a purely external kind, and that this, in its extreme form, leads to chauvinism.

Such studies show us that man's life can only be truly understood when the other side, too, is considered, that is to say, the life stretching between death and a new birth. As soon as we come to study the inner nature of man, this life between death and a new birth must be taken into consideration. For life here on the Earth is in truth a reflection of the life between death and a new birth. Life in matter is the bodily life and what we have developed in the world of spirit-and-soul before birth expresses itself in this bodily life.

What we must acquire *anew*, what must be built up anew in the core of our being, is the element appertaining to the will, and in a certain respect also to the life of feeling. The faculty of thinking that is bound up with the head—this we bring with us from the spiritual world—to the extent to which thinking is unmixed with feeling. Our thinking faculty *per se* comes with us at birth into physical existence and we have only to develop it during physical life or allow it to be developed by education. What we mainly acquire in the new incarnation through intercourse with the outer world are the qualities inherent in feeling and in will, which for this reason play an extremely important part in education.

In the sphere of education, if through our own short-comings as teachers we are incapable of helping the child to *think* properly, we may leave undeveloped much that by virtue of his previous incarnations he could have brought to expression. If, however, we are unable to work on the child's life of feeling and of will through our natural authority and our example as teachers, then we fail to impart to him what he ought to receive in the physical world, and thus we do injury to his subsequent life after death. In the modern world this is a cause of deep pain to anyone who understands these things. In the world of education to-day people insist upon the importance of the child being made to use his brain, upon the cultivation of his intellect. True, much that the child brings with him through birth is brought out by these means. But it can only be of real use when earthly life, too is presented to the child in the right way, that is to say, when we are able through example and authority to impart to him the intangible qualities belonging to feeling and to will. We injure the child's eternal life if we fail to cultivate in him the right kind of feeling and will.

The faculty of thinking which we bring with us at birth, comes to an end here, in the material world, It dies with us. Only what we cultivate through feeling and will—which is nevertheless unconsciously permeated with new thoughts—this and this only we take with us through the Gate of Death. In our present very difficult times, religion, education, indeed every domain of mental and spiritual life must begin to take account of man's *eternal* nature, not merely of human egotism.

Religions of the present day speculate far too much upon human egotism. On the one side they encourage inertia by not spurring men on to acquire those things which are eternal by inner individual effort in the life of feeling and of will ; and on the other side they enhance egotism by speaking only of eternal life after death, not of what was there before birth or conception and has come down with us into the physical world. I have said before that this life before birth is connected with *selflessness* in man, whereas human egotism comes into play whenever mention is made of the life after death. Life after death assumes an egotistic form in the religious concepts of to-day. The idea is put before man in such a way that his longings are satisfied. When the religions believe that they have helped the egotistic life of soul in man, they think they have done what is expected of them. But through a truly spiritual understanding of the world, mankind must be brought to realise how essential it is for the whole life of the human being to be viewed in the light of eternity, free from every trace of egotism and moulded accordingly by those whose task it is to teach and educate.

Now this has a significant bearing upon public life too, and it is of this that I want to speak to-day. For it is in the highest degree necessary that what we gain from an anthroposophical knowledge of higher worlds should be carried into actual life, that we should know how to bring it to expression in life. Abstract theories are really of little use. Life on the Earth is many-sided, full of variety. If, for example, we consider the life of the peoples, it is not only obvious that Indians differ from Americans or Englishmen, but Swedes are often said to differ from Norwegians although they live in such near proximity. We cannot let ourselves be guided entirely by general principles; concrete, *individual* conditions prevail everywhere and it is these that are important. It is just these individual conditions that we shall fail to recognise if we do not take our start from the Spiritual. Modern man does not really *know* the world. He talks a great deal about the world but he does not *know* it, for he is unaware that the soul-and-spirit extends into physical existence and that, fundamentally, this physical existence is governed by the Spiritual. This knowledge is not acquired by studying abstract, general principles. These abstract principles are often perfectly correct, but they do not carry us very far in the world as it actually is.

Certainly it is quite correct to say: ' God rules the world.' But in face of the manifold variety of the world it is purposeless to keep repeating : ' God rules the world in India, God rules the world in England, God rules the world in Sweden, God rules the world in Norway.' Certainly, God rules the world everywhere, but for the purposes of life in its immediate reality, it is necessary to know *how* God rules the world in India, in England, in Sweden, in Norway. In spiritual study the individual conditions must be observed in every case. Of what use would it be, for example, to take a man into a field, show him a plant with yellow flowers and round petals and merely tell him, " That is a plant "—and then take him to a plant with thorns and pointed, tapering petals, repeating : " That is a plant." It is the specific and individual properties of the plant that must be made clear to him. But in spiritual matters man has become so easy-going and slack that he is content with general principles. He only wants to hear : ' God rules the world,' or ' Man has a Guardian Angel ' and he feels no desire for detailed knowledge of how life is differentiated in the various regions of the Earth, or how its various manifestations have been influenced by the spiritual world.

This, then, will be the theme of the lecture.

It is precisely in these days of tumult, when people all over the world are so utterly at sea in public affairs, when congresses and conferences produce no result, and in spite of high-sounding programmes, men disperse without having come to any real decision—it is precisely now that deeper questions should be raised concerning all that is revealing itself from the spiritual world in the different regions of the Earth.

Think of the peninsula which you, together with the Swedes, have as your earthly dwelling-place. There is something about it that presents a kind of riddle to those who do not live in Sweden or Norway, as well as to those who actually live here. There was certainly a great difference in the way in which since 1914, let us say, you thought about the tumultuous events going on in the world. These events have struck their blows in manifold ways but man to-day is largely unaware of their effects; he does not realise what deeper forces have been and are in operation. Looking down to Middle Europe, to the South of Europe, to Africa, even to regions of Asia, the events will have seemed to you to be the direct expression of violent, elemental passions, whereas up here you were merely experiencing the consequences and reverberations of those events. People up here in the North may well have been perplexed, for it really was as though men had suddenly become frenzied with desire to tear one another to pieces. Those who were only onlookers must certainly have been perplexed when they thought about these happenings more deeply.

But such things cannot be explained by studying only the one period—even a period fraught with happenings as momentous as those of recent years. True, someone may say that it seems to him as though he had lived through centuries in these few years, but in general there will only be a very gradual realisation that this is actually so. Most people are living and thinking to-day exactly as they did in 1914. In countries like these in the North, this is in a way understandable. But that it is also the case in Middle Europe is terrible. The normal feeling would be one of having lived through events which would otherwise have come to pass only in the course of centuries. Everything was compressed into a few short years. Events like those of 1914-1915 embraced within a brief space of time as much as about ten years of the Thirty Years War, and a measure of illumination can only be shed upon them when they are studied in a much wider historical perspective.

From the vantage-point of your Northern peninsula you will be able to realise that it is only since the beginning of the present epoch that things have been happening South of you in which your participation has been different from that of the peoples who live in the South of Europe, in Western Asia, or in Middle Europe. There has really been an utter contrast between the South and the North of Europe in this respect.

I want you to think of the fourth century A.D., or rather of the period which reaches its climax in that century. In the South, on the Greek peninsula and especially on the Italian peninsula—also in the life of Middle Europe which was in contact with Italy—you see the spread of Christianity. But something else as well is to be perceived. Christianity makes its way from the East into the Pagan world of Europe, expressing itself in many different forms. When we consider the early centuries, the first, second and even the third centuries, we find the old, inherited wisdom being brought to bear upon Christianity. Efforts are made to understand Christianity through the Gnosis, as it is called, to interpret Christianity in the light of the highest form of wisdom. A change comes about in this respect, but not until the fourth century, just at the time when Christianity begins to spread more towards the regions of Middle Europe. The Gnostic conceptions, the wisdom-filled conceptions of Christianity now disappear. A writer like Origen who wants to introduce something of the old Gnostic wisdom into Christianity is branded as a heretic : Julian, the so-called Apostate, who wants to unite the old pagan wisdom with Christianity, is ostracised. And finally Christianity is externalised by the deed of Constantine into the political form of a Church. In the fourth century, that which in Christianity had once been quite different, those secrets which were felt to need the illumination of the highest wisdom if they were to become intelligible—all this begins to take on a more superficial character. Men are called upon to lay hold of Christianity in a more elementary way, with a kind of abstract feeling. Christianity makes its way from the South towards the North. It is, of course, true, that from the fourth to the fifteenth centuries, the Christian life which develops in the South and especially in Middle Europe, is rich in qualities of soul, but the Spiritual in its living essence, has receded. The Gnosis is regarded as an undesirable element in Christianity . . . There you have one or two cursory flashlights upon happenings among the peoples of Europe more towards the South.

Christianity spreads out, finds its way into the Greek world, the Roman world, into the life of Middle Europe, and there, in a certain sense it is stripped of spirituality. Think now of your Northern world in the third and fourth centuries, that is to say in the same early centuries of the post-Christian era. External history gives no true account of the conditions then prevailing. This period must be studied with the help of Anthroposophy. In connection with the European Folk-Souls this was done here some years ago (1910) but to-day we will think more of the external character of the peoples.

At the time when, in the South, the Spirit withdrew more and more towards the East—that is to say, shortly after the period I have described—the old Athenian Schools of Philosophy were closed and the last philosophers of Athens were obliged to make their way to the East, where they attached themselves to the mysterious academy of Gondi Shapur from which at that time a remarkable spiritual life was spreading via Africa and Southern Europe towards the rest of Europe, deeply influencing the spiritual life of later times. Yet it can truly be said that there, in the South, men looked back to a lofty spirituality they had once possessed. The mighty Event of Golgotha had taken place. In the first centuries it had still been found necessary to understand the Mystery of Golgotha with the help of this sublime spirituality. This spirituality had been gradually swept aside ; the *human* element had more and more taken the place of what may be called the working of the Divine in the life of man.

The Gnosis still helped man to realise the existence of the Divine-Spiritual within him. This Divine-Spiritual reality was more and more put aside and the *human* element brought to the fore. In this respect much was contributed by those peoples who took part in the migrations. In their migrations towards the South, in their conquests of the Southern regions, the Germanic peoples of Middle Europe who brought with them souls more naturally bound to the physical, contributed to this repression of the Spiritual. For they did not understand the old spirituality and brought a more fundamentally human influence to the South. And so the lofty primeval wisdom which had once been alive in men receded from the spiritual culture of the West. And at the same time when this repression of the Spiritual was taking place—in the third and fourth centuries A.D.—we find that up here in the North, teachings about the Gods were being spread among men.

In those days human beings who were inspired in an instinctive way were held in high esteem. These were times which had long since passed away for the Southern people. Up here in the North it still happened that here and there a man or a woman living in isolation would be sought out and listened to, when in a mysterious way, through faculties arising from their particular bodily constitution, they gave revelations concerning the spiritual worlds. These faculties were a natural gift in certain individuals who worked in this way among their fellows. And when the people were listening attentively to these isolated seers, they realised, when they went into the hut of one of these 'God-intoxicated,' 'God-revealing' men or women, that it was not really the physical man or woman to whom they were listening, but that it was the Divine-Spiritual itself which had descended and was inspiring such individuals in order that they might give forth the teaching of the Gods to their fellow-men.

It is very striking for the anthroposophical student of European history to find that the men of the North were still so constituted as to be able to receive divine teachings, to feel that the Gods —the Beings of the higher Hierarchies—were still living realities among them; whereas in the South, during the same period, the Spirit is becoming weaker and weaker and the *human* element which man brings to expression in his life on the physical Earth comes to the fore and supersedes the Divine. So it was in the decisive fourth century, when the men of the South were becoming more and more eager for human doctrine.

These individual revelations, springing as they did from obscure depths of spiritual life must be taken in all seriousness. It is verily as if in those times the Gods moved as teachers among the still childlike peoples of the North. This condition which was still present in a particular form in the North during the first centuries of the Christian era had long since vanished in the South. But it is a remarkable and significant fact in the destiny of the peoples that the men of the North became for the men of the South, the bearers of what had been learnt from the *Gods* —not from men.

This must be taken earnestly. The people who belonged, in the main, to the population of the West of your peninsula, whose descendants are the Norwegians of to-day, journeyed towards the West, towards the South West, and as a result of their wanderings, their sea-voyages and conquests, their influence reached right down to Sicily and North Africa The sons of the Gods. went to the sons of the World, bringing them what they had learned from their Gods.

It is an interesting chapter of history to study the migrations of the Northern peoples towards the South West and to see how—in continual metamorphosis, of course—the teachings of the Northern Gods spread towards the South West, deeply influencing the British Isles, France, Spain, Italy, Sicily and North Africa. Moreover, the effect of this influence is perceptible even to-day. The Roman, Latin form of life which makes its way from the South towards the North is permeated with the Northern influence. Whatever consciousness of the Divine has remained in the stream of civilisation from the South is here influenced by the Northern teachings of the Gods. But it takes on a peculiar character which is not fully noticeable until we look towards the Eastern side of this Northern peninsula—towards Sweden.

We need remind ourselves only of one fact—how the peoples of Eastern Europe turned to the Vareger, and how in the East of the Northern peninsula the trend is more towards the East. It is a really remarkable picture. The form of life that later on tends more towards the civilisation of Norway, streams towards the South West, and the life that later on tends towards the civilisation of Sweden, streams towards the South East. Everywhere, of course, there are the teachings of the Northern Gods, but they are presented in different ways.

The peoples who later on became the Norwegians, carry the element of activity, of strength, of enthusiasm, towards the South West. In this way the languishing Latin culture is stimulated and imbued with life. The influence of the Northern Gods in these migrations is such that it is a stimulus to activity in the whole life of the peoples. This is apparent everywhere and it is a most fascinating study.

But we also see what is happening in the East of this peninsula—It is of course influenced by geographical conditions, but these geographical conditions are also reflected in the character of the people, for the human being does not grow out of the Earth but is born on the Earth, he comes down from world of soul-and-spirit and there is a real difference between being born as a Norwegian or as a Swede. We shall not get anywhere by simply saying that the geographical conditions are such and such, but we must question further as to why one soul has the urge to become a Norwegian, and another a Swede. But now think of the remarkable character—and this applies even at the present day—of the Eastern Scandinavian, the Swedish impulses which make their way towards the East.

These impulses stream towards the East but as they advance they are everywhere deflected. They do not become really active. They cannot maintain their stand against what is brought over from the East, first by other Asiatic peoples and later by the Mongols and Tartars, nor against the early, more characteristically Eastern form of Christianity. This stream flows towards the South East but meets with obstacles everywhere and takes on a more passive character. The impulse as a whole is deeply influenced by the North. But what streams from the West of the Northern peninsula towards the South brings activity everywhere; whereas the influence that makes its way towards the East, is seized by the inactive, the more reflective element of the East and its own activity is in a way blunted.

As the Northern Gods send their impulses towards the West, they unfold, paramountly, their nature of *will*. As they send their impulse towards the East, they unfold their life of reflection, their contemplative nature.

External wars and conflicts are ultimately only the material images of what takes place in the way I have just indicated. Those who are abstract theorists, who view the whole world from the standpoint of some theory—and the empiricists of to-day are fundamentally the greatest theorists of all, for they never get down to realities, they *think about* things instead of trying to know them from inside—these theorists will bring forward all sorts of characteristics displayed by the Norwegians and the Swedes. The inhabitants of these countries themselves often emphasise the existence of outward divergencies simply because people to-day will not penetrate to the depths of human nature in order to acquire a real knowledge of life. But life must be observed in the way indicated in the two lectures I have given here. External life must be viewed not only from the standpoint of life between birth and death, but also from the standpoint of life between death and a new birth ; we must be mindful not only of those things which satisfy the egotism of the human being who merely wants to be happy after death and because he still has physical life before him, does not trouble about the life before birth. We must study how we can apply in this earthly life what we have brought with us through birth from worlds of soul-and-spirit.

Then we begin to see that there are connections in the life of men and in the life of the peoples which are only revealed when we perceive what man is and has become through many earthly lives, when we have knowledge of the periods he spends between death and a new birth.

A most remarkable connection is then revealed, helping us to understand what comes to pass on Earth. In the external national character of the Norwegian of the present day there are traits which have been inherited from those men who once migrated towards the South West and by their revelations of the Gods poured life and activity into the Roman-Latin form of civilisation. At that time something developed in the great plan of the world which gave the Norwegians their special character, their particular task. And those who are born in Norway to-day will understand their destiny and task in the world as a whole, only if they look back with spiritual understanding to the times when Norway was able to develop in a particular way, when the Northern people went forth on their migrations, their raids and their campaigns of conquest towards the South West, to fulfil a task on Earth. The task sprang out of the character of the people who inhabit these countries. Their character, it is true, was different in those times but something remains as a heritage in the present-day Norwegian and endows him with certain faculties which are important from the point of view of man's eternal life, of man's immortality.

From the Eastern part of this peninsula where the Swedish character has developed, the old teachings of the Gods were carried towards the East, to men whose own religious doctrines had been preserved in a certain mystical, oriental form. What was more a revelation from Nature met with little response in the East; those who wandered towards the East, therefore, were destined to lead a more contemplative life.

But this again has left a heritage which has set its stamp upon the character of the people. And if we are to understand the Western and the Eastern parts of the Scandinavian peninsula, we must look back to what these peoples have experienced through the centuries, realising what they have become to-day as a result of these experiences. We have every reason at the present time to think about these things. It is, after all, quite easy to realise in an elementary way that spiritual forces must be working in the world, in the whole international course of events, in the whole racial life of man, and that the missions of each particular people must be understood in the light of spiritual knowledge.

Now when the power of supersensible cognition is brought to bear upon this connection between the tasks of the modern Norwegians and Swedes and the course of their historical evolution, remarkable things come to light. Norwegians have a definite gift—nor does this gift depend upon actual birth into a Norwegian milieu. What develops in the life of Norway can be seen even in the physical world; it can be described by anthropologists, historians, or even journalists.

Their statements will be more or less correct but will give no true account of the forces at work in the depths of the human soul. For man has a mission not only here on Earth; he has a mission also in the spiritual worlds after death. And this mission in the spiritual worlds after death takes shape here, on the Earth.

What we experience in the period immediately following death is a consequence of our Earth-evolution. What we experience on the Earth immediately after birth—this again is a consequence of our life in the world of soul-and-spirit, and it is of the highest importance to study the mission of the Norwegian people not only on the Earth but in the period after death, with the means at the disposal of spiritual investigation.

Because of their physical and racial character, because of the special constitution of their brains and the rest of their bodily make-up, it can—I repeat, it *can*—fall to the lot of those souls who pass through the gate of death from the soil of the Western part of the Scandinavian peninsula, to give a very definite stimulus to other souls after death. They can give to other souls after death something that only the Norwegian characteristics are able to impart. In this epoch especially, the Norwegian character is so constituted that subconsciously and inwardly it understands *certain secrets of Nature.*

I am not now referring to your external, intellectual knowledge but to the kind of knowledge which you develop in your spiritual body, without using the physical senses, between the time of falling asleep and waking, when you are outside your bodies. When during sleep you experience the spirit in the plant-world, in stone and rock, in the rustling trees and the roaring of the waves, you become aware of the reality of forces living in the plants, hidden in the rocks, operating in the waves of the sea as they break in upon the shores, in the sparsely flowering rock-plants. A great picture arises in your souls during sleep, in the form of an intimate knowledge of Nature of which the intellect and the life of the senses are unconscious. And when, as I described in the last lecture, you develop a real connection with the Angel-Being, then you can bear into the spiritual world this unconscious Nature-wisdom, this concrete knowledge of spirituality in the plants, the stones and the other phenomena of Nature.

Those who in the true and real way have lived a Norwegian life become the stimulators and teachers of their fellow-souls after death in regard to the secrets of Nature here on the Earth. For in the spiritual world, souls must be taught about the secrets of the Earth, just as here, on the Earth, they must be taught about the secrets of the spiritual world.

In the Eastern portion of this peninsula, where the heritage from olden times is as I have described it, a different mission is carried through the gate of death. What the souls there carry through death into the spiritual world is not so much what is experienced during sleep but during waking consciousness in connection with the external world, in contemplation and study of the sense-world and in a kind of understanding—permeated with feeling—of the external world.

But this after all, is something which fundamentally speaking, has significance only for the earthly life. Yet while man is developing just this element in earthly life, something very significant develops in the subconscious region of the soul. I have pointed out to you that even in waking life a certain part of our being sleeps and dreams. The life of feeling is really only another form of dream life. In our feelings we dream and in the operations of our will we are asleep. What we know of our will is only the illumination thrown upon it by our thinking. But the kind of will that is kindled in the Swedish soul is less capable of penetrating the secrets of Nature during sleep. What enters the Swedish soul more unconsciously in the life of will and of feeling during contemplation of the outer world and in the operations of intellect and reason— that is what is carried through death. So the mission of the souls belonging to the Eastern part of the Scandinavian peninsula who pass through death is to impart to other souls an element pertaining more to the *will*—exactly the opposite of what they were able to impart to their physical fellow-beings during the times of their old historical connection with them.

Let me put it like this—A special gift in connection with the element of will developed in the Eastern part of the Scandinavian peninsula as a primary and then as an inherited quality of the character of the people. The people of Europe have lived a long time without asking in this concrete way what they really have to do after death, for they have contented themselves with the egotistical answer : We shall be happy. But if the world is to be prevented from falling into complete decadence, this egotistical answer will not suffice. It will only be possible for men to lead a true and proper life when they are willing to accept the selfless answer, when they not only ask about the happiness in store for them after death but when they also ask : What am I called upon to do, in view of my particular situation in earthly life ? Only when people are willing to frame the question in this way will they put their situation in life to proper use and so prepare truly for their mission. And then the preparation will no longer be difficult.

The two lectures—indeed the three—which I have given you here, are all connected in this respect. In view of this special mission, it is essential that the *spirituality* in the anthroposophical attitude to the world should be understood here in Norway. For when you consider that it is a specific task to create out of the subconscious life a natural science for the next world—however paradoxical this may seem, it is indeed so—then you must deliberately and consciously prepare your life of feeling in such a way that your souls, while you sleep every night, are not unreceptive to the knowledge of Nature which should be infused into them during sleep. But the bodies of to-day are not always a help in this process of preparation. The souls of the Northern peoples are, through ancient heritage, fundamentally fitted for the spiritual world. Here above all, the bodies must be influenced by a *spiritual* form of culture.

And now a great question arises which can be illuminated by comparing the mission of the peoples of Middle Europe with that of the peoples of the North.

The state of the people of Middle Europe, if they will not accept the Spiritual, was not badly described by a man who gave no thought at all to the possibility of a spiritual regeneration of humanity. Oswald Spengler has written his book on the Decline of the West, that brilliant but thoroughly pessimistic book—although he has repudiated the pessimism in a subsequent pamphlet. Of course, it is pessimism to speak of the decline of the West. But Spengler is actually speaking of the decline of culture, of something that is of the soul. Without spiritual regeneration the people of Middle Europe will suffer injury to their *souls*. But in this corner of Northern Europe, human beings cannot be injured *only* in the life of soul; when they are injured in the soul, their very bodily nature is injured at the same time. In a way this is fortunate, for if the people of Middle Europe do not accept spirituality, they become barbarian, they degenerate in *soul*. The Northern people can only die out, in the *bodily sense*, for everything depends here upon the particular constitution of the body.

The influence of a new stream of spiritual culture is profoundly necessary. For Middle Europe will degenerate, will become barbarian, will go to its decline if it does not allow itself to be influenced by the spirit. The Northerner will die out, will suffer physical death if he does not allow himself to be influenced by the Spirit.

And so what is developed here, during physical life, is connected with the mission of

Northern souls after death. They cannot fulfil their mission if they allow their bodies—which are so well-adapted for spirituality—to degenerate.

These earnest words must be uttered to-day for the evolution of our epoch demands that men shall speak together of such matters. And it is for this reason that I wanted to speak to you from the general, human standpoint, to say to you what a man says to his fellow-beings on this Earth if he has the destiny of Earth-evolution deeply at heart. For those human beings who do not prepare themselves selflessly for an eternal life, will not be leading their earthly life between birth and death aright.

That is the thought I should like to leave with you. Those who feel themselves Anthroposophists should realise that they are a tiny handful of people in the world who must apply all their energy to shaking a lazy humanity out of its lethargy and helping it onwards. Those who hate Anthroposophy to-day—this may be said among ourselves—hate it because their love of comfort and ease prevents them from being willing to grapple with the great tasks of humanity. They are afraid of what they must overcome if they are to transform their easy-going thoughts and feelings and experience something much more profound. For this reason we see many a storm of opposition arising against what is taking place in Anthroposophy and developing out of it. You too will have to accustom yourselves to violent attacks being made against Anthroposophy or Spiritual Science by reactionaries of every kind, by all who love to saunter along their old beaten tracks. Those however who let this opposition deter them from developing their powers, are not firmly rooted in the real task of Anthroposophy. When people see how Anthroposophy is being attacked to-day from all sides, they may become timid and say: Would it not be better to go forward more quietly so that the opposition may be less violent? Or again they may ask, if they find praise being meted out to them by men who in a decadent age hold leading positions: What have I done wrong? This is a matter of great importance from the anthroposophical point of view. Attacks and abuse are usually explicable for the reasons given above. But if praise were to come from the same quarters, it would be a bad augury for anthroposophical world! It is just because the opponents of Anthroposophy to-day *do* attack it, that we can be reassured—but only, of course, in the sense that we must apply all the more energy in order to introduce Anthroposophy into the world, not out of personal idiosyncracies but out of a deep realisation of the needs and tasks of the world.

On this note, then, we will conclude. Let me express to you my heartfelt thanks for your active and energetic co-operation. I assure you that I mean it seriously when I say that separation in space is no separation to those who know the reality of the spiritual bond between souls. In taking my leave, I remain together with you, I do not really go away from you. I believe you can always realise this, if you wish it to be so. You may be quite sure that there are already numbers of people who feel this bond and who look with love in their hearts towards this region in the North West with its special task—the importance of which is so well known to Anthroposophy.

I take leave of you with this love in my heart for those who feel that they truly belong to us, to our Anthroposophical Movement. May our next meeting, too, be full of the inner strength that is necessary and right among Anthroposophists.

BIBLIOGRAPHY

The ten lectures printed in this book, coinciding with the sequence on the contents page, were delivered by Rudolf Steiner in Oslo (Christiania), Norway, between November 24 and December 4, 1921.

1. November 21— Public lecture for students.
2. November 26— Public lecture for students.
3. November 28— These three public lectures
4. November 29— were delivered at the University of Christiania as a survey of Spiritual Science.
5. December 1—
6. November 29— Lecture to the Theological Association.
7. December 2— Public lecture.
8. November 24— These three lectures, to members of the branch of the Anthroposophical Society in Norway, were delivered as a unity based on a central theme.
9. November 27—
10. December 4—

www.ingramcontent.com/pod-product-compliance
Lightning Source LLC
Chambersburg PA
CBHW030334240426
43661CB00052B/1631